Behavioral Intervention Planning

Third Edition

A Comprehensive Guide for Completing a
Functional Behavioral Assessment and
Developing a Behavioral Intervention Plan

Kathleen McConnell
James R. Patton
Edward A. Polloway

8700 Shoal Creek Boulevard • Austin, Texas 78757-6897
800/897-3202 • Fax 800/397-7633 • www.proedinc.com

© 1998, 2000, 2006 by PRO-ED, Inc.
8700 Shoal Creek Boulevard
Austin, Texas 78757-6897
800/897-3202 Fax 800/397-7633
www.proedinc.com

ISBN: 1-4164-0186-5

All rights reserved. No part of the material protected by this copyright notice may be reproduced or used in any form or by any means, electronic or mechanical, including photocopying, recording, or by any information storage and retrieval system, without prior written permission of the copyright owner.

NOTICE: PRO-ED grants permission to the user of this material to copy Appendixes B, C, D, and E for school or clinical purposes. Duplication of this material for commercial use is prohibited.

Printed in the United States of America

1 2 3 4 5 6 7 8 9 10   09 08 07 06 05

Contents

Preface .... **v**

Introduction .... **vii**

Steps for Completing the Forms **1**

    Reasons and Review Form 3

    Functional Behavioral Assessment Form 9

    Behavioral Intervention Plan Form 15

    Manifestation Determination Form 21

Appendixes **27**

    A: Examples of Completed Forms 29

    B: Interventions and Strategies for Improving Students' Behavior 39

    C: Evaluation Methods 45

    D: Data-Collection Forms 47

    E: Administrative Resources 59

    F: Assessment and Instructional Resources 65

    G: Proposed Regulations 83

Preface

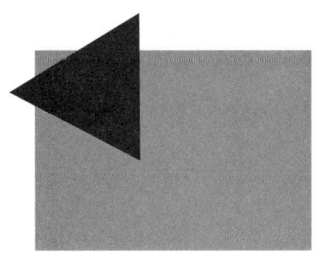

The original *Behavioral Intervention Planning* (BIP) material was developed to provide a framework for addressing the needs of students whose behaviors violated school disciplinary policies and interfered with their own or others' learning. The BIP was designed primarily for use with students identified as having a disability under the Individuals with Disabilities Education Act (IDEA; 1990), but the practices provided in this resource are appropriate also for students outside the scope of IDEA. Based on discussions with many professionals in the field who must deal with students' behavioral issues, we recognized the need for a system that is in line with the procedural mandates of IDEA and yet is still compatible with any school district's discipline policies.

The revised edition of the original BIP material, entitled BIP–R, contained some minor adjustments to the resource guide and guaranteed that the materials aligned with the regulatory language of the 1997 amendments to IDEA. This third edition of *Behavioral Intervention Planning* (BIP–3) maintains key elements of the previous editions that we feel are helpful to practitioners. The BIP–3 also includes a number of new changes to the material that are based on feedback from users of the BIP–R. Moreover, this edition incorporates all the relevant information and responds to requirements of the reauthorization of IDEA that was signed into law in December 2004.

The significant changes made in this edition include the following:

- Inclusion of relevant information from the IDEA 2004 regulations, including a flow chart to assist educators in decision making regarding disciplinary procedures
- Reorganization of the step-by-step procedures in the manual and corresponding behavioral intervention planning forms, to conform to IDEA 2004 and to streamline the Functional Behavioral Assessment and Behavioral Intervention Plan process
- Addition of observation forms that can be used to complete the Functional Behavioral Assessment
- Addition of two optional Functional Behavioral Assessment (FBA) forms: the FBA Home Version assesses students at home and thus obtains parent input, and the FBA Community Version assesses students in community settings
- Reorganization of an optional BIP Summary Sheet that can be used for communicating information to administrators and others
- Addition of an example that shows how the form could be completed for an individual with multiple behavioral issues and in whose case there was a clear change of placement issue
- Updates to the resource section to include current resources that practitioners will find helpful

Our original goal was that this manual and the accompanying forms would assist school-based personnel in dealing with the complexities associated with the significant behavioral problems displayed by certain students. As with any system such as the BIP–3, school personnel may want to modify or augment it with other district-specific materials. We have tried to make this material practical by including alternative forms, strategies for intervention, evaluation techniques, and a description of many resources—including assessments, instructional resources, and journals—that might be helpful.

We want to thank some folks whose comments, guidance, and direct assistance have helped make this material possible. We want to thank Chris Anne Worsham and Priscilla Wicker for lending invaluable skills and talents to the design of the manual and the forms as well as other production aspects of this material. We are also very appreciative of the original motivation provided by Carolyn Polloway, former Director of Special Education for Bedford County (Virginia), for opening our eyes to the need for this material. We want to thank Ed Polloway for having married Carolyn and for his contributions on earlier versions of this material. We also are grateful to the directors of special education, teachers, administrators, parents, child advocates, and attorneys (a special thank you to Jim Walsh for reviewing the manuscript) who have provided feedback regarding these materials. Many important people have played a role in this product; thanks again to all.

    KM
    JRP
    EAP

Introduction

Teachers, administrators, and other school personnel are currently faced with a multitude of issues in schools, one of the most challenging of which involves students whose behaviors significantly interfere with ongoing classroom activities and ultimately with the learning that occurs therein. The interfering behaviors may vary substantially in terms of how they look, how often they occur, or how long they last, but some will inevitably lead to school-regulated disciplinary action. Students with serious behavioral issues and the behaviors these students demonstrate create a major challenge to the instructional goals of teachers.

Many students with behavioral problems are referred to special education professionals and may receive services in either special education or general classes. It does not matter, however, where these students receive their education; if their behaviors create problems, then intervention is required. As McConnell (2001) aptly stated, "to be successful in school-based settings, some students may require behavior interventions, modifications, curriculum changes, and strategies development" (p. 1).

A key assumption in the development and use of the BIP–3 is that, to truly make significant changes to problem behaviors, one must *understand* the behavior. This means that teachers and other professionals involved in changing behavior must identify the underlying causes and functions of a behavior and analyze the existing contexts that contribute to the behaviors that are of concern. Unfortunately, most general education and special education teachers are not prepared to undertake the systematic analysis of behavior that is necessary to effect the long-lasting changes that are desired.

In addition to instructional and classroom-based considerations of why certain interfering behaviors occur, the 1997 and 2004 reauthorizations of the Individuals with Disabilities Education Act (IDEA) have emphasized the provision of protections for students with disabilities. These IDEA protections are most notable when students are subjected to a potential change of placement in conjunction with school disciplinary action resulting from a violation of the code of student conduct. Moreover, IDEA emphasizes the use of positive behavioral interventions to address the needs of students who demonstrated interfering behaviors.

To address a wide range of significant issues related to student behavior, school-based personnel need to conduct an effective and efficient Functional Behavioral Assessment (FBA) and develop an appropriate Behavioral Intervention Plan (BIP) for students whose behavior interferes with their own learning, interferes with the learning of others, or violates school disciplinary codes.

What Is a Functional Behavioral Assessment and a Behavioral Intervention Plan?

A Functional Behavioral Assessment is primarily a systematic procedure for attempting to explain why a behavior occurs by analyzing that behavior and generating hypotheses about its purpose or intended function. Ultimately, these hypotheses should assist school personnel in identifying interventions that change the student's undesirable behavior. The proposed interventions should then be documented in a plan that is shared with everyone with whom the student has contact. This document is typically referred to in IDEA as a Behavioral Intervention Plan (BIP). For students who have been determined eligible for special education, the BIP becomes part of their Individualized Education Programs (IEPs). Repp and Horner (1999) described functional behavioral assessment in the following way:

> It seeks to explain the function of the presenting problem . . . in terms of present and past environments, and then to change the environments so that appropriate behavior produces the same function, generally more efficiently and effectively, as the problem behavior had been producing. (p. 2)

The FBA and BIP process is and should be considered as a problem-solving, team-based process (McConnell, 2001). A number of individuals must contribute to conducting an FBA systematically and developing a BIP effectively. A teacher cannot successfully complete the process without assistance from other school-based personnel, parents or guardians, and, sometimes, professionals outside of school.

O'Neill et al. (1997) identified five key outcomes that should be considered when conducting an FBA:

- A clear description of the problem behavior(s).
- Identification of the events, times, and situations that predict when the problem behavior will and will not occur across the full range of typical daily routines.
- Identification of the consequences that maintain the problem behavior.
- Development of one or more summary statements or hypotheses that describe specific behaviors, a specific type of situation in which they occur, and the outcomes or reinforcers maintaining them in the situation.
- Collection of direct observation data that support the hypotheses that have been developed. (p. 3)

The BIP–3 includes components and procedures that address all five of these highlighted features.

O'Neill et al. (1997) also suggested that three techniques can be used for collecting functional behavioral assessment information. The three techniques include *informant methods* (i.e., talking with the student or others who know the student well); *direct observation* (i.e., real-time observation of the student in various contextual situations over an extended period of time); *functional analysis manipulations* (i.e., the systematic manipulation of potentially controlling variables). In reality, the first two techniques are more likely to be used in school settings than the third. When collecting functional behavioral assessment information, the following guidelines should be considered:

- During interviews, it is essential that the respondent be truly knowledgeable about the behavior in question.
- If possible, interviews should be conducted by individuals who share the student's cultural and ethnic background.
- When conducting a direct observation, it is important to use different types of observation forms, based on the type of behavior being targeted (e.g., frequency data vs. duration data).

A number of key features of the BIP should also be identified. Some of the more salient features are provided in the following list:

- The BIP should include positive interventions. IDEA does not preclude the use of punitive interventions, but the law specifies that a BIP must include positive interventions. The BIP provides a way to document positive interventions that have been identified and plans for implementation that have been generated.
- The format of the BIP should be organized so that teachers and other school-based personnel can use it easily. IDEA does not specify a format for a BIP, but goals, interventions, and methods of evaluating the effectiveness of the interventions should be clearly presented.
- Interventions will often include techniques that result in the replacement of inappropriate behaviors with appropriate behaviors; however, interventions may also include the manipulations of curriculum and environments (Hoover & Patton, 2006).
- The BIP must be shared with all school-based personnel with whom the student has contact. Adhering to this guideline is both a legal and a common sense issue; consistent application of the BIP will be impossible if this guideline is not followed.

Why and When Are FBAs and BIPs Necessary?

Subsequent to the passage of the Education for All Handicapped Children Act of 1975 (P.L. 94-142), the rights of all students with recognized disabilities were clearly affirmed by the federal government for the first time. Under P.L. 94-142 and relevant state statutes—and later under the Individuals with Disabilities Education Act of 1990 (IDEA)—students with disabilities were protected from arbitrary suspension or expulsion from school in instances in which their behavioral difficulty was determined to be related to their disability (i.e., the behavior was determined to be a manifestation of the disability). This provision was promoted as a major victory for the rights of students with disabilities because it clearly decreased the likelihood that such students could be denied a free, appropriate public education. The unforeseen result was that the protection of rights of the individual was perceived as a potential threat to school discipline in general—and to the safety and security of other students, teachers, and staff—by creating a two-tiered system of discipline.

How to administratively handle students with disabilities who demonstrate serious behavioral problems has been a controversial issue for many years. It is clear, however, that a distinct minority of students with disabilities present troublesome behaviors that challenge a school's ability to effectively educate all children and youth. As a result, when possible amendments to the IDEA were discussed beginning in the mid-1990s, a key issue was determining the appropriate balance between the rights of students with disabilities and the need for an orderly learning environment in the schools.

The legal resolution of this debate was the incorporation of a requirement for specific practices within the law. Foremost among these practices were the establishment of (a) clearer guidelines for the removal of students with disabilities from the regular school setting, (b) the need for an FBA, and (c) a requirement for the development of a BIP for individual students who present challenging behaviors within the school setting. The reauthorizations of IDEA in 1997 and 2004 reaffirmed and clarified the use of these procedures.

When IDEA was reauthorized in 1997, the quick response to the new requirements for conducting FBAs and BIPs focused on the issues of disciplinary action and change-of-placement implications for students with disabilities. Eventually it became more apparent that, although the issue of disciplinary action was indeed important and certain protections were necessary, problem behaviors of students had impacts far beyond those instances in which disciplinary action was invoked. In both the 1997 and 2004 reauthorizations of IDEA, the section of the regulations dealing with the consideration of special factors associated with the "development, review, and revision of the IEP," includes regulations that state, "in the case of a child whose behavior impedes the child's learning or that of others, consider the use of positive behavior interventions and supports, and other strategies, to address that behavior" (§ 300.324(a)(2)(i)). Obviously, addressing behaviors that impede the learning of a student or the learning of others is a far reaching and ambitious endeavor. Students who interfere with their own or others' learning are clearly more prevalent than students who face disciplinary action because of serious behavioral infractions.

We do not want to understate the importance of the procedural requirements of IDEA for conducting an FBA, determining whether the behavior in question is related to the disability, and generating a BIP when disciplinary action is invoked. We address this need in the procedural aspects of the BIP–3 and provide the regulations governing these procedures in Appendix G of this manual. However, the need to systematically analyze the functions of problematic behavior and to develop appropriate plans for intervention using positive interventions and supports is required by a large number of students in schools today. Regardless of whether the student with a behavior problem is in special education and faces disciplinary action, the use of FBAs and BIPs is warranted whenever a serious behavioral problem exists.

In our opinion, school-based or district teams should use the procedures contained in the BIP–3 in any or all of the following situations:

- As part of the prereferral intervention process

- When writing behavior plans for students served under Section 504 of the Vocational Rehabilitation Act of 1973
- To positively support students whose behavior impedes his or her learning
- To positively support students whose behavior impedes others' learning
- When required by IDEA 2004, because of long-term removal, including an Interim Alternative Educational Setting (IAES)
- When required by IDEA 2004, to conduct a Manifestation Determination

Overview of the BIP-3 Materials

Purpose

The purpose of *Behavioral Intervention Planning–Third Edition* is to outline appropriate responses to challenging behavior by suggesting how to conduct a thorough behavioral intervention planning process. To accomplish this task, forms are provided that will facilitate the process of documenting behavioral patterns and responses, evaluating the effects of previous efforts, summarizing assessment data, outlining plans, and providing a structure for evaluation. As a complement to the IEP process, these forms document the participants in the process and parental approval. By providing a framework for the behavioral intervention planning process, this material assists in effective planning, parental communication, compliance with the intents of federal regulations, and evaluation as a basis for subsequent decision making.

Specifically, the BIP-3 can be used as a framework for the following:

- Deciding when and how to intervene when students demonstrate behavior problems
- Identifying the specific reasons for conducting the behavioral intervention process
- Gathering background information that can be used to conduct an FBA
- Reviewing a prior BIP
- Conducting an FBA, including direct observation of the student, summarizing observation data, and hypothesizing about the function of the behavior
- Writing a new or modified BIP that includes effective positive interventions and supports
- Conducting a manifestation determination
- Documenting participation and consensus during the entire process

Key Components

BIP-3 is composed of two major components: this manual and four 2-page forms provided on pads. The primary function of the manual is to provide instructions for how to conduct behavioral intervention planning by using the accompanying forms and reviewing the case-study example. In addition to the background information already presented in this section, the manual offers information on the following topics:

- Descriptions of intervention strategies (see Appendix B)
- Descriptions of evaluation methods (see Appendix C)
- Sample observation forms that can be used when conducting direct observations of students (see Appendix D)
- A summary form to record disciplinary referrals that remove a student from his or her educational placement and may result in a pattern of removal (see Appendix E)
- A parent contact information form (see Appendix D)
- An administrative summary form (see Appendix E)
- An assessment and instructional resources section that can be extremely helpful in conducting this process (see Appendix F)

The forms that accompany the manual allow one to document the entire sequential process of conducting behavioral intervention planning, as described in the manual. A brief description of each form follows.

Reasons and Review

The Reasons and Review form allows school-based personnel to state the reasons why this process is being initiated. The format is easy to follow and documents essential background information.

This form provides a structured format for identifying and describing all sources of information that contribute to effective behavioral planning. The need to gather information from a variety of sources is emphasized. This information can be presented in an orderly and clear manner in this section. When completed appropriately, this section assures that proper documentation is in place.

Functional Behavioral Assessment (FBA)

The purpose of a Functional Behavioral Assessment is to provide a contextual view of the nature of specific behaviors and behavioral patterns. As such, the FBA requires professionals to understand and evaluate a behavior within the broad context of the student's home and school environments. The FBA format in the form provides a structured way to analyze the contextual aspects of a behavior by asking for an exact description of the behavior in question along with information regarding precipitating conditions, consequences that follow the behavior, and a hypothesis about the purpose or purposes the behavior serves. The form provides a link to the specific assessment techniques used to analyze the behavior as specified in the Reasons and Review form. The FBA form also allows professionals to add other qualitative information (e.g., academic, social/peer, family) that might be a factor in the demonstration of a behavior. This type of data is often overlooked in most Functional Behavioral Assessments. FBA forms designed specifically for use in the home and community are provided in Appendix D.

Behavioral Intervention Plan (BIP)

The IDEA statute and regulations similarly provide limited direction regarding the format of a BIP. Appropriate practice suggests that BIPs should include the overall goals to be achieved, interventions intended to change the student's behavior, the persons responsible for implementing the proposed interventions, and evaluation methods and timelines to be followed. The format provided in BIP form includes all of these features. To help you complete this part of the document, recommended interventions and evaluation methods are provided in Appendix B and Appendix C.

Manifestation Determination

The primary function of the Manifestation Determination form is to help to determine whether the behavior or behaviors in question are related to the student's disability. This activity is referred to in federal regulations as the "Manifestation Determination" and can be a critical aspect of the planning process. The format used in this form provides both structure and flexibility to school-based personnel. Because a Manifestation Determination is only required in very specific situations and in a limited range of circumstances, it will be helpful to review the flow chart in Appendix E to determine whether the Manifestation Determination is necessary. If the process is required, the form includes steps for conducting the Manifestation Determination and allows for documentation of that process.

The next part of the manual provides specific step-by-step procedures for completing the behavioral intervention planning forms.

References

Education for All Handicapped Children Act of 1975, 20 U.S.C. § 1400 *et seq.*

Hoover, J. J., & Patton, J. R. (2006). *Study skills instruction for students with learning and behavior problems* (2nd ed.). Austin, TX: PRO-ED.

Individuals with Disabilities Education Act of 1990, 20 U.S.C. § 1400 *et seq.*

Individuals with Disabilities Education Act Amendments of 1997, 20 U.S.C. § 1401 (26) *et seq.*

Individuals with Disabilities Education Improvement Act of 2004, 20 U.S.C. § 1400 *et seq.*

McConnell, M. E. (2001). *Functional behavioral assessment: A systematic process for assessment and intervention in general and special education classrooms.* Denver: Love.

O'Neill, R. E., Horner, R. H, Albin, R. W., Sprague, J. R., Storey, K., & Neweton, J. S. (1997). *Functional assessment and program development for problem behavior: A practical handbook.* Pacific Grove, CA: Brooks/Cole.

Repp, A. C., & Horner, R. H. (1999). *Functional analysis of behavior: From effefctive assessment to effective support.* Belmont, CA: Wadsworth.

STEPS

FOR COMPLETING THE

Forms

Reasons and Review Form ■ **3**

Functional Behavioral Assessment Form ■ **9**

Behavioral Intervention Plan Form ■ **15**

Manifestation Determination Form ■ **21**

Steps for Completing the

Reasons and Review Form

BIP-3

The Reasons and Review form should be completed by a member of the student's IEP team[1] during an IEP meeting; the team leader should read the form completely before the meeting. Team members should also gather all pertinent information and, when necessary, duplicate original material so that it is available and can be attached to this form.

Note: If prior contact with the student's parents or guardians has not been made, the team leader should call or meet with them to ensure their involvement in this process and also to obtain pertinent information on the student. Parents or legal guardians are always important members of a student's IEP team, but they do not always attend team meetings. Before initiating the behavioral intervention planning process, parent input should be sought and documented. Whenever possible, ask parents for specific information about the student's behavioral history, for the parent's suggestions for interventions, and about the effectiveness of prior behavioral plans. Parents can provide additional information by completing the FBA Home Version form in Appendix D. Information on the Parent Contact form in Appendix D should also be discussed during the IEP meeting.

After gathering the appropriate information, complete this form by thoroughly documenting the following steps.

Section One: Identifying Information

Write the name of the student, the date of the team meeting, the student's disability, the student's birth date, the student's parents' names, indication of a parent contact (check "yes" or "no") and date of contact, and the name of the meeting leader.

Mike Harris, the student in our example, is almost 13 years old. We have indicated the names of his parents and teacher, as well as the other identifying information.

---

[1] The term IEP team is used throughout this section of the manual. While the BIP-3 materials will most often be used by an IEP team, they are also appropropriate for use by 504, prereferral, or other problem-solving teams.

Section Two: Reasons for Initiating the Behavioral Intervention Planning Process

The introduction presented the background information related to the BIP process. Because the process is sometimes triggered by specific actions or by the consideration of those actions (e.g., removal of the student to another education setting), the team should closely follow the written guidelines and consult the Manifestation Determination flow chart, provided in Appendix E, before initiating the IEP meeting. To complete Section Two of the Reasons and Review form, the entire team, including parents, should discuss and agree about why the meeting is taking place, then the team recorder can check off the relevant reasons for the meeting.

Section 300.536 of IDEA 2004 explains the criteria for a change of placement under §§ 300.530 through 300.535. As of the publication date of this manual, however, the final regulations for the IDEA 2004 reauthorization were not written and so were not available. *Consult the final regulations when they are available, as this section may change.* According to this section, a change of placement occurs if

(a) The removal is for more than 10 consecutive school days; or

(b) The child has been subjected to a series of removals that constitute a pattern—

(1) Because the series of removals total more than 10 school days in a school year;

(2) Because the child's behavior, if (*sic*) substantially similar to the child's behavior in the incidents that resulted in the series of removals, taken cumulatively, is determined, under §300.530(f), to have been a manifestation of the child's disability; and

(3) Because of such additional factors as the length of each removal, the total amount of time the child has been removed, and the proximity of the removals to one another. (20 U.S.C. 1415 (k))

You must examine information related to removals to determine whether they are part of a series that constitutes a pattern. This information should be recorded and reviewed before beginning the meeting. To assist you in the review, a Discussion Guide and a Removal Record form are provided in Appendix E. There are no "one size fits all" guidelines for determining that a series of removals constitutes a pattern; each student's information should be reviewed individually. Carefully consider all pertinent facts before coming to a conclusion. In Section 300.536 of IDEA 2004, the inclusion of the word *and* implies that all three of the criteria listed must be met in order for the series of removals to constitute a pattern. Use caution and common sense when making a decision about the cumulative impact of removals from an educational placement. In addition, you should seek legal counsel if any questions remain regarding whether a series of removals constitutes a pattern.

Reasons for Initiating the Behavioral Intervention Planning Process

✔ The student demonstrates a pattern of behavior problems that interferes with his or her learning.

✔ The student demonstrates a pattern of behavior problems that interferes with others' learning.

✔ The student *has violated the student conduct code,* and removal to an Interim Alternative Educational Setting (IAES), another setting, or suspension is being considered or has occurred. The removal would be
  ✔ more than 10 school days.
  ☐ 10 school days or fewer (no BIP required).
  ☐ part of a series of removals that totals more than 10 school days in a school year and that constitutes a pattern. (See p. 60 for an explanation of a series of removals constituting a pattern.)

☐ The student has been removed to an Interim Alternative Educational Setting (IAES) for up to 45 school days for a violation involving weapons, drugs, or infliction of serious bodily injury, *without regard to whether or not behavior is a manifestation of the disability.*

SECTION two

In our example, Mike's behavior has interfered with his own and with others' learning.

STEP 3

Section Three: Review of Prior BIP or Other Behavioral Interventions

Completion of this section is required for a long-term change of placement if a student has a prior BIP in place and if the student's behavior is a manifestation of his or her disability. It is good practice to review prior behavioral plans before writing a new BIP as part of a comprehensive functional behavioral assessment. Completion of Section Three of the Reasons and Review form requires the team to identify interventions that were included in the prior plan. There is space on the form to review a total of 12 interventions, three in each of the intervention categories: Positive Environmental Supports, Instructional Strategies, Positive Reinforcement, and Reductive Consequences; however, we recommend reviewing a smaller number of interventions, including those used most often and those found to be most or least effective. The team should indicate the frequency with which the interventions were used and then rate their effectiveness as *not effective*, *somewhat effective*, or *very effective*. A review of past interventions can help the team make decisions about what interventions to include in the next BIP.

SECTION three

Review of Prior Behavioral Intervention Plan (BIP) or Other Behavioral Interventions

Prior BIP in effect? ✔ Yes ☐ No   Attached? ✔ Yes ☐ No
Other plan in effect? ☐ Yes ✔ No   Attached? ☐ Yes ☐ No

If no prior behavioral plan is in effect, skip this section.

Dates of prior BIP or plan: From 4/10/05 To 4/10/06
Targeted Behaviors/Goals: Comply with requests
Decrease verbal aggression

Interventions Implemented*	Frequency (D = daily, M = monthly, W = weekly, N = as needed)	Not Effective	Somewhat Effective	Very Effective
Positive Environmental Supports				
Behavior contract	D	☐	✔	☐
Seating near teacher	D	☐	✔	☐
Instructional Strategies				
Positive Reinforcement				
Contract points can be used to "purchase" time to listen to music		☐	☐	✔
Praise and high-fives		✔	☐	☐
Reductive Consequences				
Loss of points	N	✔	☐	☐
Call to parents	N	☐	✔	☐
Detention	N	✔	☐	☐

*There is space for review of three behavior interventions in each intervention category. However, we suggest that you limit your review to the most commonly used interventions.

In our example, Mike's prior BIP included several interventions, some of which seemed to be ineffective or only somewhat effective. Only one intervention (music time) was very effective.

Steps for Completing the

Functional Behavioral Assessment Form

BIP–3

The Functional Behavioral Assessment (FBA) form should be completed when the Functional Behavioral Assessment is conducted. The IEP team members should read the form completely before discussing it during an IEP meeting. Team members should also gather all pertinent information and, when necessary, duplicate original material so that it is available and can be attached to this form. The FBA form includes space for the team to record background information summaries, but it is often helpful to have the complete reports or records for reference.

Section One: Background Information

The purpose of this section is to ensure the collection and review of information related to the student's behavior. The IEP team may wish to complete the Parent Contact form and observation forms in Appendix D before meeting. In addition, behavior checklists or rating scales that are to be considered should be completed and then scored or summarized before the meeting. The team should discuss and review the information obtained and then attach the original information. Because many students with serious behavioral problems have a long history of behavioral infractions, the team may choose to include only recent records.

To complete the form, the team leader should write the student's name at the top and check each box next to the background information that the team discusses and considers relevant to the student's behavior. Parents should be given an opportunity to provide additional information and insight into their child's history and current performance.

BIP–3 | **9**

Behavioral Intervention Planning–Third Edition

BIP-3

Functional Behavioral Assessment (FBA)

Steps for completing this form can be found on pages 9 through 13 in the manual.

Student's Name: __Mike Harris__

In our example, Mike has a history of misbehavior, so there is a lot of information for the team to consider. The team will discuss information from Mike's parents, his observation data, discipline records, assessment information, and a review of his prior Behavior Intervention Plan (BIP).

Background Information
The following sources of background information were considered for this FBA.

✔ Parent information/interview (see Parent Contact form) — Attached? ✔ Yes ☐ No
Summary of parent information: Mike's parents have had problems with him at home. They think positive approaches work best.

☐ Behavior checklist or rating scale — Attached? ☐ Yes ☐ No
Summary of checklist or rating scale:

✔ Recent observation data (see data collection forms) — Attached? ✔ Yes ☐ No
Summary of observations: Frequency data from math observation indicated that Mike follows only about half of teacher directions.

✔ Discipline records — Attached? ✔ Yes ☐ No
Summary of discipline records: Five referrals this semester.

✔ Assessment information — Attached? ✔ Yes ☐ No
Summary of assessment information: Mike is learning disabled (LD) in math and emotionally disturbed (ED).

☐ Information from other agencies or service providers — Attached? ☐ Yes ☐ No
Summary of other information:

✔ Review of prior BIP (see Reasons and Review form, Section Three) — Attached? ✔ Yes ☐ No
Summary: Music is a motivator. Detention not working.

☐ Student interview/conference — Attached? ☐ Yes ☐ No
Summary:

☐ Video- or audiotape — Attached? ☐ Yes ☐ No
Summary:

☐ Teacher/administrator interview(s) — Attached? ☐ Yes ☐ No
Summary:

SECTION one

Section Two: Analysis of Behavior

When completing Section Two of the FBA form, the IEP team should consider one behavior at a time. The form has a blank space for the behavior number (i.e., Prioritized Behavior # ___) and a blank space for a description of the behavior, because only one behavior should be considered at a time, and a separate page should be completed for each behavior.

Select the first behavior for assessment and write it on the form.

The first behavior targeted for assessment should be the most serious behavior that interferes with the student's or anothers' learning that has resulted in possible removal to a more restrictive environment. Describe the behavior as is typically described by school personnel and parents.

Student's Name: __Mike Harris__

Analysis of Behavior
Prioritized Behavior # __1__   __Following directions__

Antecedents (Events or conditions occurring before or triggering the behavior)	Behavior* (Exactly what the student does or does not do)	Consequences (Actions or events occurring after the behavior)	Function of Behavior (Hypothesized purpose of the behavior)

☐ Setting, subject, or class:	Behavior in observable, measurable terms: _Refuses to follow directions, ignores, says "no," argues_	☐ Behavior is ignored
		  ☐ Planned
		  ☐ Unplanned
			✔ Avoidance or escape
			  ✔ Avoid a directive or request
			  ✔ Avoid an assignment
			  ☐ Escape a situation or a person

☐ Time of day:		✔ Peer attention	

☐ Person(s):	Baseline measures of behavior	✔ Adult attention
		  ✔ Reminder(s)
		  ✔ Repeated directive or request
		  ✔ Private meeting or conference
		  ✔ Reprimand or warning
			☐ Attention
			  ☐ Gain peer attention
			  ☐ Gain adult attention

☐ Interruption in routine:	Frequency of behavior: _50% of requests_ ___ per ___		☐ Self-control issue
			  ☐ Express frustration
			  ☐ Express anger
			  ☐ Vengeance
			  ☐ Power or control
			  ☐ Intimidation

✔ Directive or request to: _begin an assigment_	Duration of behavior: ___ per incident	☐ Change in directive or request	

☐ Consequences imposed:	Intensity of behavior:	☐ Loss of privilege:
		☐ Time out in classroom
			☐ Sensory or emotional reaction
			  ☐ Fear or anxiety
			  ☐ Sensory relief or stimulation

In our example, Mike's first behavior is *following directions*.

BIP-3 | 11

Complete the first column, *Antecedents*.

The first column of Section Two is intended to identify the antecedents (events or situations that occur before the behavior and may trigger its occurrence). Several choices are provided, including the setting, time of day, persons, and events. There is also space for *other* antecedents that are not listed. Indicate that there is more than one antecedent for the behavior by checking more than one box.

Complete the second column, *Behavior*.

The team should identify exactly what the student does or does not do in observable, measurable terms, then provide baseline information (i.e., the observed frequency, duration, or intensity of the behavior). To obtain reliable baseline information, the staff should observe or collect data on the behavior for at least 2 to 3 weeks.

In Mike's case, his refusal to follow directions occurs after he is given a directive or request to do something, especially when the directive involves a difficult task, and he is likely to become frustrated. The first column on Mike's form shows two checks, one for *Directive or Request to begin an assignment* and one for *Difficulty or Frustration involving assignments*.

Antecedents (Events or conditions occurring before or triggering the behavior)	Behavior* (Exactly what the student does or does not do)
☐ Setting, subject, or class:	Behavior in observable, measurable terms: **Refuses to follow directions, ignores, says "no," argues**
☐ Time of day:	
☐ Person(s):	Baseline measures of behavior
☐ Interruption in routine:	Frequency of behavior: **50% of requests** _____ per _____
✓ Directive or request to: **begin an assigment**	Duration of behavior: _____ per incident
☐ Consequences imposed:	Intensity of behavior:
☐ Lack of social attention:	
✓ Difficulty or frustration: **with assignments**	
☐ Other(s):	

In our example, when Mike refuses to follow directions, he ignores, says "no," or argues and does not follow a directive to begin his work. He responds this way after approximately 50% of the directives given to him by his teachers.

*Observation forms for collecting data are available in Appendix D.

Complete the third column, *Consequences.*

The team should identify the observed consequences of the behavior and check the corresponding boxes. If other consequences occur, check the "Other(s)" box and list them. It is important that the team identify consequences that actually occur, whether the team intends for them to occur or not. For example, peer attention often occurs after misbehavior and may be a very powerful consequence. Teachers may not realize that peer attention is occurring, however, and consequently may not understand its role in maintaining the behavior. Completing this section of the form will be more accurate if background information is gathered through observations, audio- or videotapes, or other reliable tools.

Complete the final column, *Function of Behavior.*

This is an important section of the form and requires discussion by the IEP team because it is a hypothesis, not a fact. However, lasting, meaningful behavior change will be difficult unless the purpose of the student's behavior is identified. The team should check off the items that describe the hypothesized purpose or function of the behavior. The team will have to design other interventions that either help the student achieve his or her purpose in a more appropriate way or assure the student that achieving his or her purpose cannot be allowed and will result in serious consequences.

In our example, Mike's behavior is typically followed by several consequences: peer attention, adult attention (including reminders, repeated directives, private meetings), reprimands, and detention assigned by an administrator.

Consequences (Actions or events occurring after the behavior)	**Function of Behavior** (Hypothesized purpose of the behavior)
☐ Behavior is ignored ☐ Planned ☐ Unplanned	✔Avoidance or escape ✔Avoid a directive or request ✔Avoid an assignment ☐ Escape a situation or a person
✔Peer attention	
✔Adult attention ✔Reminder(s) ✔Repeated directive or request ✔Private meeting or conference ✔Reprimand or warning	☐ Attention ☐ Gain peer attention ☐ Gain adult attention
☐ Change in directive or request	☐ Self-control issue ☐ Express frustration ☐ Express anger ☐ Vengeance ☐ Power or control ☐ Intimidation
☐ Loss of privilege:	☐ Sensory or emotional reaction ☐ Fear or anxiety ☐ Sensory relief or stimulation
☐ Time out in classroom	☐ Other(s):
✔Administrative consequences:	
☐ Parent contact	
☐ Other(s):	

In Mike's case, the team believes that the purpose of his behavior is clearly to avoid directives and assignments, especially when they are difficult for him, as in math class.

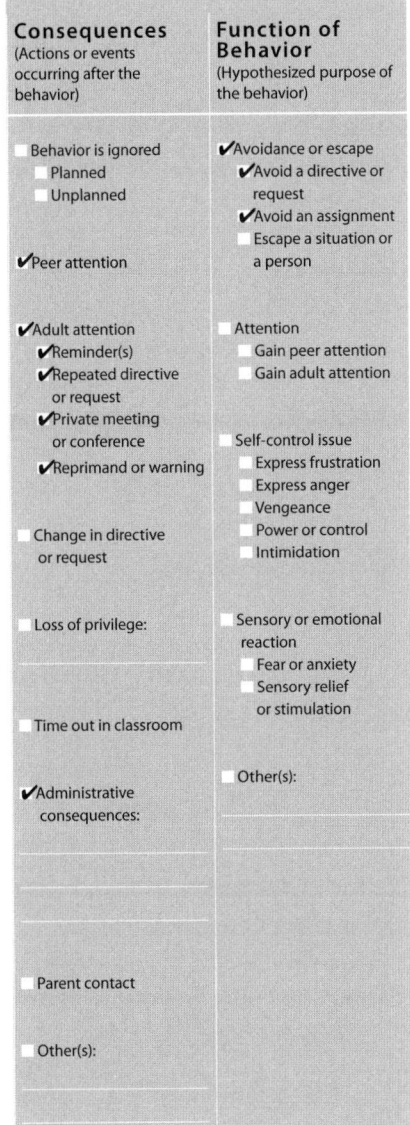

Steps for Completing the

Behavioral Intervention Plan Form

BIP-3

The Behavioral Intervention Plan (BIP) form should be completed when writing a student's Behavioral Intervention Plan. IEP team members should read the form completely and be prepared before discussing it during a meeting.

Before completing the BIP form, the team should complete the Reasons and Review form and the Functional Behavioral Assessment form. Section Three on the Reasons and Review form should provide information essential to writing the BIP. This review is intended to help everyone on the team evaluate the effectiveness of prior interventions. Conducting a thoughtful review of prior plans can help prevent unnecessary discussion of intervention options that are unlikely to improve the student's behavior.

In addition, it will be helpful for everyone on the team to consult the interventions and strategies in Appendix B. This list, which is divided into four sections that correspond to the four categories in Section Three of the BIP form, provides a number of suggestions for practical and effective interventions. Note that all students are subject to the student conduct code (SCC). Short-term disciplinary consequences that do not involve a change of placement may be imposed for any SCC violation. For example, students are often assigned to lunch detention for minor infractions. This SCC consequence does not require IEP team approval. The planning will go more quickly if each member of the team comes to the meeting with suggestions as well as concerns. Preparation should also ensure that the plan developed will significantly affect the student's behavior.

Finally, the IEP committee should also review the evaluation methods presented in Appendix C. Every Behavioral Intervention Plan should include a timeline for evaluation and should state the methods that will be used in that evaluation. If team members are not familiar with options for evaluation, Appendix C will provide some useful ideas.

Behaviors

Only one behavior at a time should be considered, and a separate BIP form should be completed for each behavior. The pages can then be combined to address several behaviors if the team feels that such a plan is required. Usually, the first behavior selected for intervention on the BIP will be the first behavior targeted in Section Two of the Functional Behavioral Assessment form. When writing the BIP, however, the committee should decide exactly what behavior will be targeted for a decrease and what behavior will be taught as a replacement behavior. It is important to include a replacement behavior whenever possible so that the committee's focus remains on teaching and increasing positive behaviors. Occasionally, there may be a unique situation that requires only a behavior decrease, but as a rule, a positive replacement behavior should always be the focus of intervention.

Behavioral Intervention Planning–Third Edition

BIP–3

Behavioral Intervention Plan (BIP)

Steps for completing this form can be found on pages 15 through 19 in the manual.

Student's Name: **Mike Harris**

In our example, the team will address two behaviors, shown at the top of the BIP form. First, in Behavior To Be Decreased, the committee would like to decrease Mike's refusal to follow directions, especially his refusal to begin assignments. Second, in Replacement Behavior, the behavior the committee would like to increase has two parts: Say "okay", and begin when directed to do so.

Behavior # **1** Behavior To Be Decreased: **Refuse to follow directions**
Replacement Behavior: **Say "okay" and begin**

Specific Behavioral Objective	Interventions*	Person(s) Responsible	Evaluation Method(s)/Timeline
Mike will: Say "okay" and begin assignment within 2 minutes	Positive environmental supports: Contract, Visual cues, Partner for assignments	Teachers will: Use contract, provide visual cues, assign partners	Method(s): Check grades for zeroes, Review contract with Mike, Contact parents

Columns

Complete the first column, *Specific Behavioral Objective*.

Write the student's name in the first blank, and complete the other blanks by describing the conditions and criteria for the behavior.

First, describe the conditions under which the team would like the behavior to be demonstrated (or not demonstrated, in some cases). These can include descriptions of the following:

- Setting (e.g., math class)
- Type of directive (e.g., verbal)
- Degree of support (e.g., independent)
- People involved (e.g., peers)
- Time limits (e.g., within 1 minute)
- Materials involved (e.g., a visual reminder)
- Other conditions related to performance of the behavior

It is important to write realistic conditions that all staff members understand and feel comfortable including.

Next, decide on the criteria for the behavior. *Criteria* are the standards that must be met for mastery of the behavioral objective. Criteria are necessary so that the team will know if and when the student meets the objective. Criteria should also be realistic and will be more accurate if baseline data have been collected, as was discussed in the directions for completing the Functional Behavioral Assessment form. Baseline data and all of the other information discussed during the FBA process will assist the team in determining criteria. Criteria can include the following:

- A percentage or fraction (e.g., 70% of the time or half of the opportunities available)
- A total frequency or rate (e.g., three times per day)
- A duration measure (e.g., for at least 10 minutes)
- An increase or improvement rate (e.g., from a baseline of once per hour to five times per hour)

Again, the team should be realistic about the criteria; criteria that require unrealistic improvements in behavior are unlikely to be effective.

Specific Behavioral Objective

Mike

will:
Say "okay" and begin assignment within 2 minutes

under these conditions:
When given a verbal direction

To meet these criteria:
Improve from 50% to 80% of time

Our example shows that the behavioral objective for Mike is as follows: Mike will say "okay" to his teachers and follow their spoken directions within 2 minutes. The team has set a criterion of 80% (Mike must respond this way to 80% of his teachers' directions). This criterion represents a significant improvement from Mike's current rate (50%) of direction following.

Complete the second column, *Interventions*.

The second column of the BIP form provides space to write interventions in four categories: Positive Environmental Supports, Instructional Strategies, Positive Reinforcement, and Reductive Consequences. As was mentioned previously, suggestions for specific interventions in each of these four categories can be found in Appendix B. To ensure a well-rounded plan that has a high probability of working, the committee should consider several interventions. The plan *must* include positive strategies and supports, not just reductive consequences.

Complete the third column, *Person(s) Responsible*.

Write the names of the persons responsible for implementing the BIP. Without a clear assignment of responsibilities, many BIPs are not implemented consistently and, as a consequence, are not effective. In order to assure thorough implementation, the team should assign individuals to specific responsibilities. We suggest that, whenever possible, students and their parents be assigned responsibilities to ensure student and parental involvement.

In our example, Mike will be supported by a contract for following directions, responding to visual reminder cues, and working with a partner for some assignments. Mike will also be given a repetition of directions and an extra example. He will have his choice of a positive reinforcer if his direction-following behavior reaches the 80% criterion. If Mike reaches the 80% goal and maintains it for at least 2 weeks, his father has agreed to take him to a nearby NASCAR track to watch a race. At school, Mike will earn points for early music time and early lunch. Consequences will include making up his work before school or a lunch detention.

Interventions*	Person(s) Responsible
Positive environmental supports: Contract Visual cues Partner for assignments	Teachers will: Use contract, provide visual cues, assign partners
Instructional strategies: Repeat directions Provide an extra example	Principal will: Administer detention
Positive reinforcement: Points for music time or early lunch, home reward—car races	
Reductive consequences:** Make up work before school Lunch detention	Mr. Harris will: Reward Mike with a trip to the car races

Mike's BIP requires that his teachers monitor his contract in conference with Mike; the principal, who will administer detention; and Mike's father, who will reward Mike with a trip to the racetrack if his behavior improves. In our example, the team effort is very evident.

Complete the last column, *Evaluation Method(s)/Timeline.*

Appendix C lists several evaluation methods that range from summaries of behavior evaluation forms or contracts to a review of student attendance. It is important for the team to decide on these evaluation methods at the time the BIP is written so that the data required for the evaluation are collected for the implementation of the plan. When deciding on the evaluation methods, team members should again review who is responsible for collecting specific information so that at the end of the evaluation period all data are available.

> **Evaluation Method(s)/Timeline**
>
> Method(s):
> Check grades for zeroes
> Review contract with Mike
> Contact parents
>
> Timeline:
> 2 weeks, 4 weeks, 6 weeks

Mike's team decided to evaluate his progress at the end of 2 weeks, 4 weeks, and 6 weeks after implementing the BIP. Reviews will include a teacher–student progress review and a summary and graph of Mike's percentage of following directions. The team suggested that Mike do the graphing himself so that he understands and takes credit for his progress. The team will also check Mike's grades to determine if he has any zeroes acquired for incomplete work. Finally, the team will speak to Mike's parents to see if any changes in Mike's attitude were noticed and to find out if he has earned his trip to the racetrack.

Additional Information

STEP 3

The bottom of the form has a small section that allows the team to explain any unique circumstances related to the student. This brief response was included because IDEA 2004 allows the IEP committee to consider unique circumstances when they are conducting a Manifestation Determination for specific students. Not all students will be subject to a manifestation determination, but the inclusion of information about unique circumstances may assist the team in case a manifestation determination is at some point required.

> Additional information: **Mike has a secondary diagnosis of emotional disturbance.**
>
> * Interventions must include positive behavior supports (positive environmental supports and positive reinforcement). The BIP may not contain only reductive consequences.
> ** All students are subject to the student code of conduct (SCC). Short-term disciplinary consequences that do not involve a change of placement may be imposed for any SCC violation.

In Mike's case, the team has pointed out his secondary diagnosis of emotional disturbance (ED). The ED diagnosis may or may not be related to some of his refusals to follow directions. During a Manifestation Determination, the team may or may not decide that the ED diagnosis has *caused* or has had a *substantial relationship* to specific behaviors.

Steps for Completing the

Manifestation Determination Form

BIP-3

The Manifestation Determination form should be completed only when determining whether a student's behavior is a manifestation of his or her disability. Before beginning the Manifestation Determination process, it may be helpful to review the Manifestation Determination flow chart in Appendix E, which will assist the team in following all steps required by IDEA 2004. Because the Manifestation Determination must be conducted only when a placement change of more than 10 school days is being considered, many students will never require this portion of the behavioral intervention planning process. However, when a change of placement of more than 10 school days is being considered, the IEP team must complete the entire Manifestation Determination.

Because IDEA 2004 requires a review of all relevant information provided by teachers, parents, and others as part of the Manifestation Determination, the Reasons and Review, Functional Behavioral Assessment, and Behavioral Intervention Plan forms should all be reviewed if they are part of the student's records. This review will provide invaluable information as to whether a specific behavior is the manifestation of the student's disability. After thoroughly reviewing all of the information, including specific behavioral data, the team members should read the Manifestation Determination form completely before discussing it during the meeting.

Section One: Identifying Information

Write the name of the student, his or her disability, parents' names, and the teacher or leader of the meeting. Also indicate the date of the meeting, the student's date of birth, and whether or when the parents were contacted.

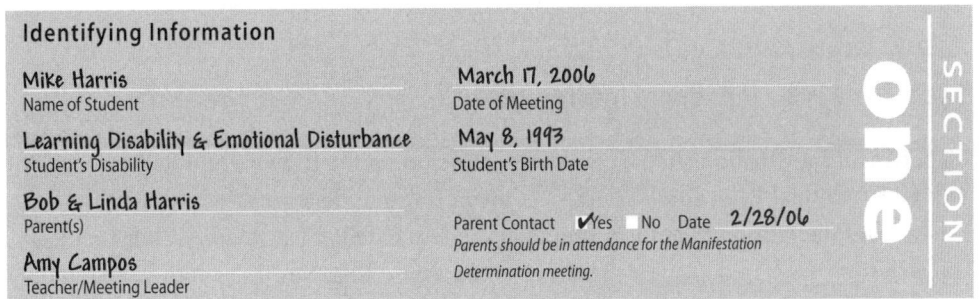

In our example, Mike's identifying information is the same as on the Reasons and Review form, but the date of the meeting is different.

STEPS

Section Two: Reasons for Meeting

In Section Two, the team should be able to easily decide whether the situation that requires a Manifestation Determination has occurred. If the answer to Question 4, 5, or 6 is "yes," then a Manifestation Determination is required. A "yes" response to any of these questions means that a placement change of more than 10 school days is being considered.

Section 615(k) of IDEA 2004 allows school personnel to consider unique circumstances on a case-by-case basis when deciding whether to order a change in placement. Question 7 addresses this point.

Section Three: Description of the Student's Conduct That Violated the Student Code of Conduct

The team should briefly describe the student's conduct code violation in this section. The description should be as clear as possible, including action verbs that tell exactly what the student did. If there is an incident report, it should be discussed and attached.

Section Four: Proposed Disciplinary Action

In Section Four, the team should describe the recommended disciplinary action. Remember that the Manifestation Determination process is used only for changes in placement of more than 10 school days.

Section Five: Review of Information

All pertinent information should be reviewed, including the Reasons and Review form and the Functional Behavioral Assessment form. If the student already has a BIP, then the Behavioral Intervention Plan form should also be included in the review of information. For each item discussed, place a check in the corresponding "yes" box on the form. If information listed is not discussed, check the "no" box. Other information can be discussed and should be noted on the blank line at the end of the section.

Reasons for Meeting

✔Yes	☐No	1. Has the student violated the student code of conduct? *If the answer to number 1 is yes, continue to answer the questions below.*
☐Yes	✔No	2. Is a placement change to an Interim Alternative Educational Setting (IAES), another setting, or suspension for **not more than 10 school days** being considered or already been ordered?
☐Yes	✔No	3. Is such a placement change (**not more than 10 school days**) applied to a student without a disability for the same violation of the student code of conduct? *If the answers to both question 2 and question 3 are yes, a Manifestation Determination is not necessary.*
✔Yes	☐No	4. Is a placement change to an IAES, another setting, or suspension for **more than 10 school days** being considered? *If the answer to question 4 is yes, conduct a Manifestation Determination.*
☐Yes	✔No	5. Is a placement change to an IAES, another setting, or suspension that is part of a series of removals totaling **more than 10 school days** and constituting a pattern being considered? (See p. 60 for an explanation of a series of removals constituting a pattern.) *If the answer to question 5 is yes, conduct a Manifestation Determination.*
☐Yes	✔No	6. Is a placement change to an IAES for **not more than 45 school days** for a violation involving weapons, drugs, or infliction of serious bodily injury? *If the answer to question 6 is yes, conduct a Manifestation Determination.**
☐Yes	✔No	7. Are there any unique circumstances for this student that were considered when deciding whether to order a change in placement? *If so, explain:* _____

*When violations involve weapons, drugs, or serious bodily injury, the student may be removed to an IAES for not more than 45 school days, without regard to whether the behavior is a manifestation of the disability.

SECTION two

In Mike's case, he has violated the student code of conduct, and a change in placement for more than 10 school days is being considered.

Description of the Student's Conduct That Violated the Student Code of Conduct

Mike became angry in math class and threw a chair at his teacher, Ms. Ravelle.

✔Yes ☐No Incident report attached?

SECTION three

In our example, Mike became angry and threw a chair at his math teacher, which is noted in this section of the form.

Proposed Disciplinary Action

The team is considering a placement of 20 school days in the district's alternative placement.

SECTION four

Mike's team is considering a placement of 20 school days in the district's alternative placement.

Review of Information (Must Include IEP, Teacher Observation, Parent Information)

Check "yes" if the information is reviewed by the IEP committee during the manifestation determination meeting and "no" if it is not.

✔Yes ☐No Reasons and Review Form (Section Three, Review of Prior BIP)
✔Yes ☐No Individualized Education Program (IEP)
✔Yes ☐No Functional Behavioral Assessment Form
            (Section One, Background Information, and Section Two, Analysis of Behavior)
✔Yes ☐No Behavioral Intervention Plan (BIP) Form
✔Yes ☐No Other: Counseling report

SECTION five

In Mike's case, the IEP team reviewed all of the information listed and also reviewed a report from the school counselor.

BIP-3 | 23

STEP 6

Section Six: Conclusions of IEP Committee

Section Six is the most important part of the Manifestation Determination form and represents the specific answer to the Manifestation Determination question. The IEP committee, after reviewing all relevant information, should answer Questions 1, 2, and 3. Question 1 asks about the relationship between the student's conduct and his or her disability. It is important to note that IDEA 2004 requires that the student's conduct be caused by, or have a direct and substantial relationship to, the child's disability if it is to be considered a manifestation of the disability. This is a much more stringent standard than in IDEA 1997, which addressed only the issue of a connection between the behavior and the disability. Question 2 asks if the conduct was a direct result of the school district's failure to implement the IEP. The committee should review the IEP to ensure that it was implemented. If the IEP was not implemented, the committee should then determine whether the student's conduct was a direct result of that failure.

- If the answer to either Question 1 or 2 is "yes," the conduct is considered a manifestation of the student's disability, and Question 3 should be checked "yes."

- If the answer to both questions is "no," the conduct is not a manifestation of the disability and the answer to Question 3 is "no."

Mike's team answered "no" to all three questions, indicating that his conduct was not a manifestation of the disability.

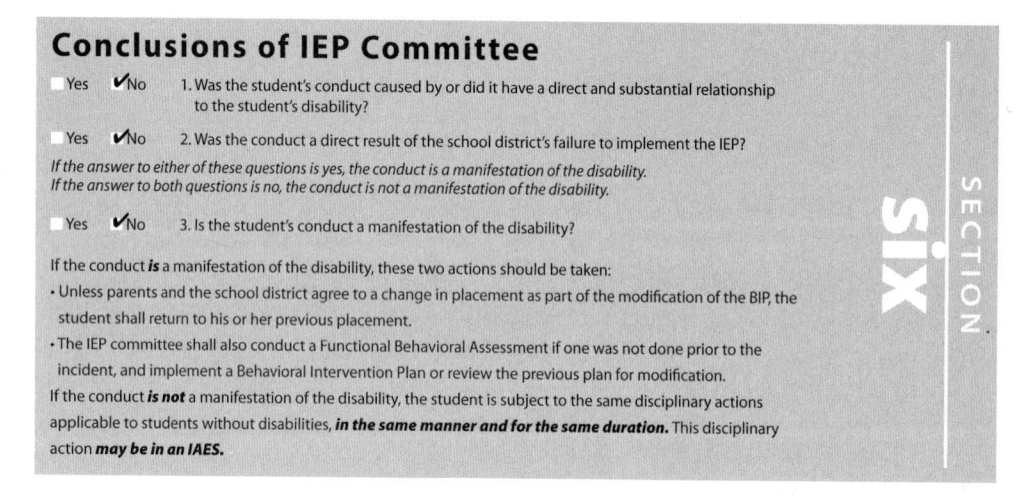

Conclusions of IEP Committee

☐ Yes ☑ No 1. Was the student's conduct caused by or did it have a direct and substantial relationship to the student's disability?

☐ Yes ☑ No 2. Was the conduct a direct result of the school district's failure to implement the IEP?

If the answer to either of these questions is yes, the conduct is a manifestation of the disability.
If the answer to both questions is no, the conduct is not a manifestation of the disability.

☐ Yes ☑ No 3. Is the student's conduct a manifestation of the disability?

If the conduct **is** a manifestation of the disability, these two actions should be taken:
- Unless parents and the school district agree to a change in placement as part of the modification of the BIP, the student shall return to his or her previous placement.
- The IEP committee shall also conduct a Functional Behavioral Assessment if one was not done prior to the incident, and implement a Behavioral Intervention Plan or review the previous plan for modification.

If the conduct **is not** a manifestation of the disability, the student is subject to the same disciplinary actions applicable to students without disabilities, **in the same manner and for the same duration.** This disciplinary action **may be in an IAES.**

SECTION six

STEP 7

Section Seven: Signatures and Indication of the IEP Committee Members

Section Seven is designed to record the signatures of each member of the IEP committee and to document their agreement with the answer to Question 3 in Section Six. Although individual responses are not required in the statute, we recommend that this section be completed by the entire team to ensure unanimity regarding the decision and to prevent later challenges to the decision.

Signatures and Indication of the IEP Committee Members
Check "yes" if you believe the student's conduct is a manifestation of his disability and "no" if you do not believe the student's conduct is a manifestation of his or her disability.

- ☐ Yes ☑ No — Amy Campos—lead teacher
- ☐ Yes ☑ No — Betty Ann Ravelle—math teacher
- ☐ Yes ☑ No — Linda Harris—mother
- ☐ Yes ☑ No — Kelly Marse—principal
- ☐ Yes ☑ No — Maureen Downs—psychologist
- ☐ Yes ☑ No — Frank Bertelli—counselor

Everyone on Mike's team agreed that his behavior was not a manifestation of his disability.

APPENDIXES

A: Examples of Completed Forms **29**
  Reasons and Review 30
  Functional Behavioral Assessment 32
  Behavioral Intervention Plan 35
  Manifestation Determination 37

B: Interventions and Strategies for Improving Students' Behavior. **39**

C: Evaluation Methods **45**

D: Data-Collection Forms **47**
  Descriptive Behavior 50
  Behavior Duration 51
  Behavior Frequency 52
  Behavior Comparison 53
  Behavior Tracker 54
  Behavior Purpose 55
  Parent Contact 56
  Functional Behavioral Assessment (FBA) Home Version 57
  Functional Behavioral Assessment (FBA) Community Version .. 58

E: Administrative Resources **59**
  Discussion Guide: Series of Removals That Constitute a Pattern 60
  Removal Record 61
  Manifestation Determination (Flow Chart) 62
  Administrator's Summary of Behavioral Intervention Plan (BIP) 64

F: Assessment and Instructional Resources **65**
  Assessment Instruments 65
  Instructional Resowurces 68
  Journals 81

G: Proposed Regulations **83**

Examples of Completed Forms

APPENDIX A

Behavioral Intervention Planning–Third Edition

BIP–3

Reasons and Review

Steps for completing this form can be found on pages 3 through 7 in the manual.

SECTION one

Identifying Information

Name of Student: Mike Harris

Student's Disability: Learning Disability & Emotional Disturbance

Parent(s): Bob & Linda Harris

Teacher(s)/Meeting Leader: Amy Campos

Date of Meeting: March 17, 2006

Student's Birth Date: May 8, 1993

Parent Contact ✔Yes ☐No Date 2/28/06

SECTION two

Reasons for Initiating the Behavioral Intervention Planning Process

✔ The student demonstrates a pattern of behavior problems that interferes with his or her learning.

✔ The student demonstrates a pattern of behavior problems that interferes with others' learning.

✔ The student *has violated the student conduct code,* and removal to an Interim Alternative Educational Setting (IAES), another setting, or suspension is being considered or has occurred. The removal would be
  ✔ more than 10 school days.
  ☐ 10 school days or fewer (no BIP required).
  ☐ part of a series of removals that totals more than 10 school days in a school year and that constitutes a pattern. (See p. 60 for an explanation of a series of removals constituting a pattern.)

☐ The student has been removed to an Interim Alternative Educational Setting (IAES) for up to 45 school days for a violation involving weapons, drugs, or infliction of serious bodily injury, *without regard to whether or not behavior is a manifestation of the disability.*

SECTION three

Review of Prior Behavioral Intervention Plan (BIP) or Other Behavioral Interventions

Prior BIP in effect? ✔ Yes ☐ No Attached? ✔ Yes ☐ No
Other plan in effect? ☐ Yes ✔ No Attached? ☐ Yes ☐ No

If no prior behavioral plan is in effect, skip this section.

Dates of prior BIP or plan: From 4/10/05 To 4/10/06
Targeted Behaviors/Goals: Comply with requests
Decrease verbal aggression

Interventions Implemented*	Frequency D = daily M = monthly W = weekly N = as needed	Effectiveness Not Effective / Somewhat Effective / Very Effective
Positive Environmental Supports		
Behavior contract	D	☐ / ✔ / ☐
Seating near teacher	D	☐ / ✔ / ☐
		☐ / ☐ / ☐
Instructional Strategies		
		☐ / ☐ / ☐
		☐ / ☐ / ☐
		☐ / ☐ / ☐
Positive Reinforcement		
Contract points can be used to "purchase" time to listen to music		☐ / ☐ / ✔
Praise and high-fives		✔ / ☐ / ☐
Reductive Consequences		
Loss of points	N	✔ / ☐ / ☐
Call to parents	N	☐ / ✔ / ☐
Detention	N	✔ / ☐ / ☐

*There is space for review of three behavior interventions in each intervention category. However, we suggest that you limit your review to the most commonly used interventions.

BIP-3

Behavioral Intervention Planning–Third Edition

BIP–3

Functional Behavioral Assessment (FBA)

Steps for completing this form can be found on pages 9 through 13 in the manual.

Student's Name: __Mike Harris__

Background Information
The following sources of background information were considered for this FBA.

- ☑ Parent information/interview (see Parent Contact form)   Attached? ☑ Yes ☐ No
  Summary of parent information: __Mike's parents have had problems with him at home. They think positive approaches work best.__

- ☐ Behavior checklist or rating scale   Attached? ☐ Yes ☐ No
  Summary of checklist or rating scale: _____

- ☑ Recent observation data (see data collection forms)   Attached? ☑ Yes ☐ No
  Summary of observations: __Frequency data from math observation indicated that Mike follows only about half of teacher directions.__

- ☑ Discipline records   Attached? ☑ Yes ☐ No
  Summary of discipline records: __Five referrals this semester.__

- ☑ Assessment information   Attached? ☑ Yes ☐ No
  Summary of assessment information: __Mike is learning disabled (LD) in math and emotionally disturbed (ED).__

- ☐ Information from other agencies or service providers   Attached? ☐ Yes ☐ No
  Summary of other information: _____

- ☑ Review of prior BIP (see Reasons and Review form, Section Three)   Attached? ☑ Yes ☐ No
  Summary: __Music is a motivator. Detention not working.__

- ☐ Student interview/conference   Attached? ☐ Yes ☐ No
  Summary: _____

- ☐ Video- or audiotape   Attached? ☐ Yes ☐ No
  Summary: _____

- ☐ Teacher/administrator interview(s)   Attached? ☐ Yes ☐ No
  Summary: _____

SECTION one

Student's Name: __Mike Harris__

Analysis of Behavior

Prioritized Behavior # __1__   __Following directions__

Antecedents (Events or conditions occurring before or triggering the behavior)	Behavior* (Exactly what the student does or does not do)	Consequences (Actions or events occurring after the behavior)	Function of Behavior (Hypothesized purpose of the behavior)
☐ Setting, subject, or class: _____	Behavior in observable, measurable terms: __Refuses to follow directions, ignores, says "no," argues__	☐ Behavior is ignored 　☐ Planned 　☐ Unplanned	✔ Avoidance or escape 　✔ Avoid a directive or request 　✔ Avoid an assignment 　☐ Escape a situation or a person
☐ Time of day: _____		✔ Peer attention	
☐ Person(s): _____	Baseline measures of behavior Frequency of behavior: __50% of requests__ per _____	✔ Adult attention 　✔ Reminder(s) 　✔ Repeated directive or request 　✔ Private meeting or conference 　✔ Reprimand or warning	☐ Attention 　☐ Gain peer attention 　☐ Gain adult attention
☐ Interruption in routine: _____			☐ Self-control issue 　☐ Express frustration 　☐ Express anger 　☐ Vengeance 　☐ Power or control 　☐ Intimidation
✔ Directive or request to: __begin an assigment__	Duration of behavior: _____ per incident	☐ Change in directive or request	
☐ Consequences imposed: _____	Intensity of behavior: _____	☐ Loss of privilege: _____	☐ Sensory or emotional reaction 　☐ Fear or anxiety 　☐ Sensory relief or stimulation
☐ Lack of social attention: _____		☐ Time out in classroom	☐ Other(s): _____
✔ Difficulty or frustration: __with assignments__		✔ Administrative consequences: _____	
☐ Other(s): _____		☐ Parent contact ☐ Other(s): _____	

SECTION two

* Observation forms for collecting data are available in Appendix D.

Student's Name: __Mike Harris__

Analysis of Behavior

Prioritized Behavior # __2__ __Verbal aggression__

Antecedents
(Events or conditions occurring before or triggering the behavior)

- ✔ Setting, subject, or class: __math class__
- ☐ Time of day:
- ☐ Person(s):
- ☐ Interruption in routine:
- ☐ Directive or request to:
- ☐ Consequences imposed:
- ☐ Lack of social attention:
- ✔ Difficulty or frustration: __math assignments__
- ☐ Other(s):

Behavior*
(Exactly what the student does or does not do)

Behavior in observable, measurable terms:
__Threatens, yells and curses at teacher__

Baseline measures of behavior
Frequency of behavior:
__2 times__ per __class__

Duration of behavior:
_____ per incident

Intensity of behavior:
__Escalates to loud yelling, moves too close to teacher__

Consequences
(Actions or events occurring after the behavior)

- ☐ Behavior is ignored
  - ☐ Planned
  - ☐ Unplanned
- ☐ Peer attention
- ✔ Adult attention
  - ☐ Reminder(s)
  - ☐ Repeated directive or request
  - ✔ Private meeting or conference
  - ✔ Reprimand or warning
- ✔ Change in directive or request
- ☐ Loss of privilege:
- ✔ Time out in classroom
- ✔ Administrative consequences: __Removal from class Detention__
- ✔ Parent contact
- ☐ Other(s):

Function of Behavior
(Hypothesized purpose of the behavior)

- ✔ Avoidance or escape
  - ✔ Avoid a directive or request
  - ✔ Avoid an assignment
  - ☐ Escape a situation or a person
- ☐ Attention
  - ☐ Gain peer attention
  - ☐ Gain adult attention
- ✔ Self-control issue
  - ☐ Express frustration
  - ✔ Express anger
  - ☐ Vengeance
  - ✔ Power or control
  - ✔ Intimidation
- ✔ Sensory or emotional reaction
  - ✔ Fear or anxiety
  - ☐ Sensory relief or stimulation
- ☐ Other(s):

SECTION two

* Observation forms for collecting data are available in Appendix D.

Behavioral Intervention Planning–Third Edition

BIP-3

Behavioral Intervention Plan (BIP)

Steps for completing this form can be found on pages 15 through 19 in the manual.

Student's Name: __Mike Harris__

Behavior # __1__ Behavior To Be Decreased: __Refuse to follow directions__
Replacement Behavior: __Say "okay" and begin__

Specific Behavioral Objective	Interventions*	Person(s) Responsible	Evaluation Method(s)/Timeline
Mike will: Say "okay" and begin assignment within 2 minutes under these conditions: When given a verbal direction To meet these criteria: Improve from 50% to 80% of time	Positive environmental supports: Contract Visual cues Partner for assignments Instructional strategies: Repeat directions Provide an extra example Positive reinforcement: Points for music time or early lunch, home reward—car races Reductive consequences:** Make up work before school Lunch detention	Teachers will: Use contract, provide visual cues, assign partners Principal will: Administer detention Mr. Harris will: Reward Mike with a trip to the car races	Method(s): Check grades for zeroes Review contract with Mike Contact parents Timeline: 2 weeks, 4 weeks, 6 weeks

Additional information: __Mike has a secondary diagnosis of emotional disturbance.__

* Interventions must include positive behavior supports (positive environmental supports and positive reinforcement). The BIP may not contain only reductive consequences.

** All students are subject to the student code of conduct (SCC). Short-term disciplinary consequences that do not involve a change of placement may be imposed for any SCC violation.

Behavioral Intervention Planning–Third Edition

BIP-3

Behavioral Intervention Plan (BIP)

Steps for completing this form can be found on pages 15 through 19 in the manual.

Student's Name: __Mike Harris__

Behavior #: __2__
Behavior To Be Decreased: __Verbal aggression__
Replacement Behavior: __Express feelings without threatening__

Specific Behavioral Objective	Interventions*	Person(s) Responsible	Evaluation Method(s)/Timeline
Mike will: Express a complaint or frustration without verbal threats under these conditions: In math class To meet these criteria: 100% of time	Positive environmental supports: Visual cue to calm down; Bonus points on contract Instructional strategies: Anger management class Positive reinforcement: Music time; Early lunch; Call parents Reductive consequences:** Lunch detention; In-school suspension	Math teacher will: Cue Mike; Use contract; Call parents Counselor will: Provide anger management class Mike will: Attend anger management class, practice new ways to express feelings	Method(s): Check discipline referrals; Review contract; Conference with Mike Timeline: 2 weeks, 4 weeks, 6 weeks

Additional information:

* Interventions must include positive behavior supports (positive environmental supports and positive reinforcement). The BIP may not contain only reductive consequences.

** All students are subject to the student code of conduct (SCC). Short-term disciplinary consequences that do not involve a change of placement may be imposed for any SCC violation.

Behavioral Intervention Planning–Third Edition

BIP-3
Manifestation Determination
Steps for completing this form can be found on pages 21 through 25 in the manual.

Identifying Information — SECTION one

Mike Harris
Name of Student

Learning Disability & Emotional Disturbance
Student's Disability

Bob & Linda Harris
Parent(s)

Amy Campos
Teacher/Meeting Leader

March 17, 2006
Date of Meeting

May 8, 1993
Student's Birth Date

Parent Contact ✔Yes ☐No Date 2/28/06
Parents should be in attendance for the Manifestation Determination meeting.

Reasons for Meeting — SECTION two

✔Yes ☐No 1. Has the student violated the student code of conduct?
If the answer to number 1 is yes, continue to answer the questions below.

☐Yes ✔No 2. Is a placement change to an Interim Alternative Educational Setting (IAES), another setting, or suspension for **not more than 10 school days** being considered or already been ordered?

☐Yes ✔No 3. Is such a placement change **(not more than 10 school days)** applied to a student without a disability for the same violation of the student code of conduct?
If the answers to both question 2 and question 3 are yes, a Manifestation Determination is not necessary.

✔Yes ☐No 4. Is a placement change to an IAES, another setting, or suspension for **more than 10 school days** being considered?
If the answer to question 4 is yes, conduct a Manifestation Determination.

☐Yes ✔No 5. Is a placement change to an IAES, another setting, or suspension that is part of a series of removals totaling **more than 10 school days** and constituting a pattern being considered? (See p. 60 for an explanation of a series of removals constituting a pattern.)
If the answer to question 5 is yes, conduct a Manifestation Determination.

☐Yes ✔No 6. Is a placement change to an IAES for **not more than 45 school days** for a violation involving weapons, drugs, or infliction of serious bodily injury?
If the answer to question 6 is yes, conduct a Manifestation Determination.*

☐Yes ✔No 7. Are there any unique circumstances for this student that were considered when deciding whether to order a change in placement?
If so, explain:

*When violations involve weapons, drugs, or serious bodily injury, the student may be removed to an IAES for not more than 45 school days, without regard to whether the behavior is a manifestation of the disability.

Description of the Student's Conduct That Violated the Student Code of Conduct — SECTION three

Mike became angry in math class and threw a chair at his teacher, Ms. Ravelle.

✔Yes ☐No Incident report attached?

BIP–3 | 37

SECTION four

Proposed Disciplinary Action

The team is considering a placement of 20 school days in the district's alternative placement.

SECTION five

Review of Information (Must Include IEP, Teacher Observation, Parent Information)
Check "yes" if the information is reviewed by the IEP committee during the manifestation determination meeting and "no" if it is not.

- ✔Yes ☐No — Reasons and Review Form (Section Three, Review of Prior BIP)
- ✔Yes ☐No — Individualized Education Program (IEP)
- ✔Yes ☐No — Functional Behavioral Assessment Form
  (Section One, Background Information, and Section Two, Analysis of Behavior)
- ✔Yes ☐No — Behavioral Intervention Plan (BIP) Form
- ✔Yes ☐No — Other: Counseling report

SECTION six

Conclusions of IEP Committee

- ☐Yes ✔No — 1. Was the student's conduct caused by or did it have a direct and substantial relationship to the student's disability?
- ☐Yes ✔No — 2. Was the conduct a direct result of the school district's failure to implement the IEP?

If the answer to either of these questions is yes, the conduct is a manifestation of the disability.
If the answer to both questions is no, the conduct is not a manifestation of the disability.

- ☐Yes ✔No — 3. Is the student's conduct a manifestation of the disability?

If the conduct **is** a manifestation of the disability, these two actions should be taken:

- Unless parents and the school district agree to a change in placement as part of the modification of the BIP, the student shall return to his or her previous placement.
- The IEP committee shall also conduct a Functional Behavioral Assessment if one was not done prior to the incident, and implement a Behavioral Intervention Plan or review the previous plan for modification.

If the conduct **is not** a manifestation of the disability, the student is subject to the same disciplinary actions applicable to students without disabilities, **in the same manner and for the same duration.** This disciplinary action **may be in an IAES.**

SECTION seven

Signatures and Indication of the IEP Committee Members:
Check "yes" if you believe the student's conduct is a manifestation of his disability and "no" if you do not believe the student's conduct is a manifestation of his or her disability.

- ☐Yes ✔No — Amy Campos—lead teacher
- ☐Yes ✔No — Betty Ann Ravelle—math teacher
- ☐Yes ✔No — Linda Harris—mother
- ☐Yes ✔No — Kelly Marse—principal
- ☐Yes ✔No — Maureen Downs—psychologist
- ☐Yes ✔No — Frank Bertelli—counselor

BIP–3

APPENDIX B

Interventions and Strategies for Improving Students' Behavior

The example provided for each strategy is intended only as an illustration of how the strategy might be used.

These examples are not intended to represent an inclusive list of strategies.

Positive Environmental Supports

1. **Remove distracting materials**
   If Bryan plays with his keys instead of doing his work, Mr. Janus removes the keys.

2. **Provide a quiet, separate seating area**
   When Chris has a difficult time focusing his attention, Mrs. Cunningham asks him to move to a study carrel, away from noise.

3. **Modify academic requirements**
   If Cecelia gets upset when she gets a full page of math problems to do, Ms. Taliaferro gives her only five problems at a time.

4. **Use visual cues/signals/advance organizers**
   When Darnell is frustrated, Ms. Wood flashes a signal card that says "Help is on the way."

5. **Provide written or visual schedule**
   To keep Andrew on track, Ms. Reinhart uses a picture symbol schedule.

6. **Use proximity cues**
   When JaNiece gets loud and agitated, Ms. Rule moves closer to her (i.e., stands about 3 feet away).

7. **Provide choices related to assignments**
   To provide independent practice of a taught skill, Ms. Young lets Maricella choose from a number of activities.

8. **Use gestures, physical cues**
   To let Kim know she is talking out too much, Mrs. Fountain uses a subtle "shhh" sign (finger to lips).

9. **Minimize transition time**
   Mr. Bonilla keeps a separate schedule for Henry so that when he finishes his work he knows that he can start his independent contract, work on the computer, or read a book.

10. Structure group supports
Janelle and Teresa check each other's assignment book every afternoon.

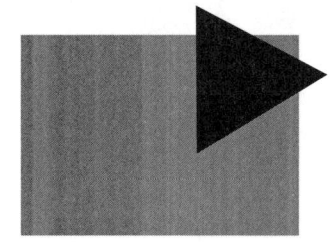

11. Other: _____
_____

Instructional Techniques

1. Teach class rules or procedures, and establish expectations or set limits
Ms. Garza teaches a direct-instruction lesson on her rules and procedures, including examples and nonexamples and an assessment of understanding.

2. Model desirable behavior
Ms. Giles demonstrates exactly how she wants her students to ask for help.

3. Use strategic placement
In the cafeteria, Mr. Harris seats Jimmy near some students whose behavior is usually acceptable and positive.

4. Role-play
After providing Byron with an example of the correct behavior, Mr. Templeton asks him to demonstrate for the rest of the class the correct way to respond to teasing.

5. Coach through use of corrective feedback
After Joe demonstrates how to express a complaint, Mrs. Stevenson tells him exactly what he did right, what he did wrong, and how to do it better next time.

6. Provide literature-based lessons
Ms. Timmons uses a book about friendship to help Louise learn how to make new friends.

7. Monitor and provide written feedback
Mr. Graves sends home a daily report that indicates Ray's behavior performance in class.

8. Develop student–teacher contract
Andre and Mrs. Jones sign an agreement stating that if Andre turns in three homework assignments, Mrs. Jones will give him a coupon for one night off from homework.

9. Develop student–parent contract
Juan and his parents sign a written contract stating that Juan will get to go to the bike rodeo if he averages 80% on his daily behavior form.

10. Teach self-monitoring
Mr. Smith teaches Tom how to self-record his talk-outs on a form attached to his desk.

11. Show and discuss videotapes
Mr. Hahn shows a video on anger control and self-management, then leads a discussion on the techniques.

12. Use team-building activities
Ms. Livingston goes through a 1-day ROPES course with her class.

13. Provide social skills games
Mr. Contreras plays a board game with Jeannie that focuses on problem-solving skills in social situations.

14. Organize group discussions
Ms. Lin leads a class discussion on ways to resist peer pressure.

15. Other: _____
_____

Positive Reinforcement

1. Use frequent, consistent, specific verbal praise
Every time George says, "Okay," when asked to correct his work, Mr. Kelly says, "Good job, George. I appreciate it when you respond positively to a request."

2. Provide positive social reinforcement
Each time Horatio walks down the hall without yelling, Ms. Salazar smiles at him and gives him a high five.

3. Establish point system
Mr. Bullis uses points to record appropriate performance on Mike's daily check sheet.

4. Establish in-class or in-school reward system
At Washington Middle School, students trade in behavior points for rewards like posters, time in the sports room, or movie passes.

5. Establish home–school reward system
Mr. and Mrs. Thomas agree to provide Sandra with a small stuffed toy for her collection each week that her behavior meets the teacher's 80% criterion.

6. Establish token economy
Ms. Bancroft's students collect stamps in a book for positive behaviors, then trade them in for items with specific prices listed in a catalog.

7. Refer to other adults for praise
Each day that Tawni comes to school on time, her teacher lets her stop and get a pat on the back from the principal, Ms. Beaver.

8. Use privileges/responsibilities
When Francine talks politely to the principal, she is allowed to deliver messages from the office.

9. Use private praise
Mr. Blackstock meets with Rochelle privately and compliments her for her progress.

10. Use random drawings
Ms. Henry provides tickets for her students when they complete assignments. On Friday, she picks three tickets and gives prizes to the students whose names are on them.

11. Provide tangible reinforcement
If Marcello finishes all of his assignments, he earns an item that is important to him (e.g., a baseball cap).

12. Provide consumable reinforcement
If Darren does not swear during group discussion, Mr. Morris gives him a Power Bar or Gatorade.

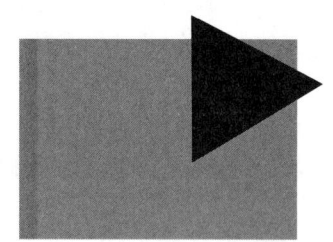

13. Other: _____
_____

Reductive Consequences
Positive support interventions should always be implemented first, if possible.

1. Implement previously agreed behavior contract
Michael has been on time to class every day for 2 weeks, so Mr. Jamal provides him with a pass for 2 extra hours of Internet access. If he is late for class, though, he loses minutes of computer time.

2. Use reinforcement techniques for lower rates of behavior
Ms. Bailey provides reinforcement for Alton when he meets a lower criterion of cursing by continuing to lower the criterion.

3. Use nonverbal signals
When Saundra breaks a class rule twice in a row, Ms. Rendell first moves her warning card from green to yellow, then from yellow to red.

4. Provide verbal reminder or reprimand
When Jason refuses to follow a direction, Ms. Myers reminds him that the class rules require him to comply with the requests of adults.

5. Set up system of planned ignoring *(This must be used in conjunction with the establishment of appropriate replacement behaviors.)*
During class discussion, Andrea talks out without raising her hand. Mr. Franklin continues the discussion, calling on and recognizing only those students who raise their hands before talking.

6. Use a structured warning system

Mr. Netathumen uses posted numbers to count down from 5 to 1, giving Mandy visual warnings before he gives her a consequence.

7. Assign essays or writing assignments

When Alonzo curses in class, Mr. Graves requires that he write a thoughtful essay explaining what he did, why it is unacceptable, and what he will do differently next time.

8. Use cost response procedures

Kristen starts the day with six tokens, and Ms. Crowe takes one away each time Kristen criticizes someone else. If Kristen has any tokens left at the end of the day, she can *buy* an activity.

9. Provide time to cool off at desk or other area

When Scott loses at a game of checkers and starts to complain loudly, Ms. Ramirez asks him to move to the quiet corner.

10. Implement loss of privileges

When Jonas runs in the hall, he is no longer the line leader.

11. Arrange student–teacher conference

During her conference period, Ms. Liu meets privately with Donald to discuss his disrespectful behavior.

12. Refer to counselor or mentor

Mr. McDougal refers LaVel to the school counselor when he notices that LaVel is becoming increasingly withdrawn and depressed.

13. Telephone parent(s)

Ms. Babbitt calls Janelle's parents to let them know that Janelle is cursing in class.

14. Administrative consequences for violations of student code of conduct

_____
_____
_____
_____
_____

Evaluation Methods

APPENDIX C

1. **Behavior monitoring forms (e.g., contracts, point sheets)**
   Forms that can be used for managing behavior include behavioral contracts that are negotiated between the student and teacher and sheets that are used for indicating the points students receive for demonstrating appropriate behaviors.

2. **Grades for assignments recorded in grade book**
   Grades for class assignments or activities are typically recorded in a location (i.e., grade book) that can be consulted for ongoing performance information.

3. **Anecdotal notes**
   Anecdotal notes represents any type of note-taking that is developed to describe ongoing behaviors. Anecdotal formats vary greatly, representing the specific needs of the situation or the person taking the notes. Anecdotal notes are sometimes referred to as "narrative reports" or "continuous recording."

4. **Attendance records**
   Any system that personnel implement to record the attendance (e.g., at school, in class) of a student. Computer systems are sometimes used for this purpose.

5. **Tally sheets or hand-held counter of the frequency of target behavior(s)**
   One of the most commonly used systems for recording the number of times a certain behavior or set of behaviors are observed. (A form for collecting frequency data is available in Appendix D.) Golf counters or grocery-store counters can also be used.

6. **Progress reports or interim notices**
   Progress reports provide an ongoing appraisal of the progress associated with behaviors and intervention programs. They can be issued on a more regular basis than grades—which are typically given at the end of a 9-week grading period—and be generated by a variety of different school-based personnel.

7. **Portfolios and work samples**
   Portfolios and work samples comprise any variety of student products. Sometimes portfolios represent a student's best work; other times they include a sampling of all work that has been generated. This methodology can be used in conjunction with other evaluation techniques.

8. **Student self-assessments or ratings**
   Checklists or rating scales that allow students to evaluate their own behavior and record their beliefs about their behaviors according to established criteria can be used.

9. Teacher or parent rating scales

Such rating scales typically include a list of statements related to various behaviors or conditions along with a range of choices completed by teachers and parents. Rating scales given to parents must be written in a manner that is easily understood.

10. IEP review forms

IEP review forms provide longitudinal information related to the goals and objectives established in an IEP. Typically, these forms are used to review student performance when IEP meetings are held.

11. Parent feedback forms

Home–school communication is a system that requests information from parents on target behavior(s). A format that helps structure the feedback increases the chances that communication between parents and teachers is clear, thus preventing misunderstandings.

12. Time totals on stopwatches

To determine how long a behavior exists or how long it takes for a student to demonstrate a desired behavior requires a time measurement. All variations of how behavior demonstrations are collected (i.e., live vs. taping) require some type of timing system, such as a stopwatch.

13. Graphing behavioral performance

Graphing represents one of the best methods for displaying the ongoing behavioral performance due to its visual format. Computer software (e.g., Microsoft Excel) simplifies this task significantly and provides attractive displays. Students can graph their own progress.

14. Observation data

Data collected through use of forms should be reviewed regularly. Reproducible forms are provided in Appendix D.

15. Other: _____
_____

APPENDIX D

Data-Collection Forms

This appendix includes data-collection forms for observations and parent contacts, and forms for completing a home FBA and a community FBA. They are easy to use, and directions are provided for the first six forms.

Descriptive Behavior (p. 50)

1. Write the name of the student and the behavior being observed at the top of the page.

2. Next, write the steps or components of the behavior in the lines at the top of the grid. For example, if the behavior is a tantrum, the components might include hitting, spitting, yelling, throwing things, and crying.

3. In the left-hand column of the grid, write the date of each observation. During the observation, put a checkmark in the box(es) under the specific components of the behavior that are observed. One way to measure progress is to determine if fewer (in the case of a tantrum) or more (dealing with frustration appropriately) behaviors are observed and checked on the grid.

Behavior Duration (p. 51)

1. Fill in the information at the top of the page, including the student's name, the date, and the behavior being observed.

2. Each time the behavior begins, write down the start time. When the behavior ends, write down the stop time.

3. Subtract the start time from the stop time, and write the time elapsed during the behavior (i.e, its duration).

4. To compute the average of the recorded durations, add the times and divide by the number of observations.

Behavior Frequency (p. 52)

1. Write the student's name and the behavior you are observing at the top of the page.

2. Write the date of the observation and the name of the observer in the first and second columns, respectively.

3. In the third column, Time, write the time of the observation. This can be either the start and stop times or the total amount of time spent observing. Use column four to make tally marks every time the behavior occurs.

4. In the fifth column, write the total number of times the behavior occurred during the observation period.

5. In the sixth column, Rate, compute the rate of the behavior by dividing the number of times it occurred by the total amount of time elapsed.

6. Write any relevant comments in the last column.

Behavior Comparison (p. 53)

This observation form allows the observer to record the behavior of two students, one the subject of the observation and the other a comparison student. It is intended to allow for frequent observations at regular intervals and is perfect for observing on-task behavior. Here are the steps to complete the form.

1. Write the names of the students, the date, the class or time of day, and the target behavior on the top of the form. If you do not know the name of the comparison student (Student B), put a description (male) or a pseudonym (Bob).

2. Before writing the times in the first column, decide how often during the observation you are going to observe and record. This could be every 2 minutes, every 5 minutes, every 10 minutes, and so forth. After making this decision, write the times on the form (e.g., 9:00, 9:05, 9:10).

3. Record whether you see the target behavior exhibited by student A and by student B at the same time. You may wish to code the behavior by writing a "+" if you observe the behavior and a "−" if you do not. You may either record using an interval process, which means the behavior occurred *during* the interval, or record the behavior if it occurrs at the specific time of observation.

4. Use the last column to write any pertinent notes or more detailed descriptions.

Behavior Tracker (p. 54)

This form allows for a quick and easy frequency count of how many times a behavior is observed during 10 opportunities or trials. Here are the steps to complete the form.

1. Write the name of the student and behavior being observed at the top.

2. Start at the bottom and move up the column. Color in or cross out a box each time you observe the behavior.

3. In the oval at the top of each column, write the total number of times you observed the behavior during the 10 trials. At the bottom of the column, write the date.

4. When you are finished, you should have a graph representing the number of times the behavior occurred when 10 opportunities were provided each day for 5 days.

Behavior Purpose (p. 55)

1. Write the name of the student and the date at the top of the form.

2. In the first column, Time/Setting, write the time of your observation and the setting (e.g., lunch time or language arts class).

3. In the second column, Observer, write the observer's name.
4. In the third column, Description of Behavior, write the behavior that you are observing (e.g., talking out, getting out of seat).
5. Under Purpose of Behavior, check one or more of the five columns to indicate the purpose of the behavior. If you are not sure of the purpose, hypothesize, take your best guess.
6. Write any relevant comments in the last column.

Observation Record

Descriptive Behavior

BIP-3

Name: _____ Behavior: _____

Behavior Components or Steps

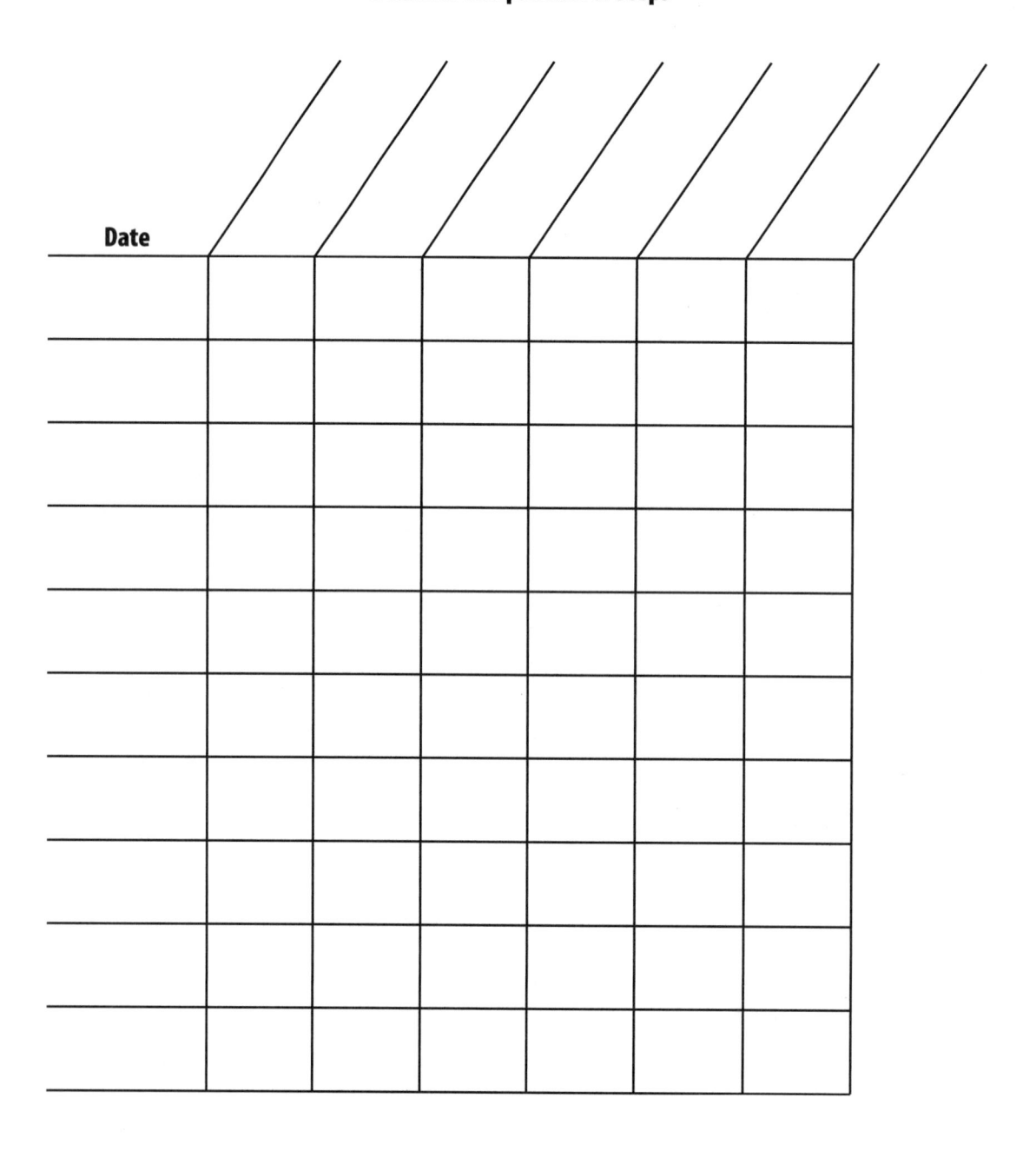

Date						

© 2006 by PRO-ED, Inc.

Observation Record

BIP–3

Behavior Duration

Name: _____   Date: _____

Behavior: _____

Trial		
1	Stop Time	_____ : _____
	Start Time	_____ : _____
	Duration	_____ : _____
2	Stop Time	_____ : _____
	Start Time	_____ : _____
	Duration	_____ : _____
3	Stop Time	_____ : _____
	Start Time	_____ : _____
	Duration	_____ : _____
4	Stop Time	_____ : _____
	Start Time	_____ : _____
	Duration	_____ : _____
5	Stop Time	_____ : _____
	Start Time	_____ : _____
	Duration	_____ : _____
	Average Duration	_____ : _____

© 2006 by PRO-ED, Inc.

Observation Record
Behavior Frequency

Name: _____ Behavior: _____

DATE	OBSERVER	TIME	FREQUENCY	TOTAL	RATE	COMMENTS
					____ per ____	
					____ per ____	
					____ per ____	
					____ per ____	
					____ per ____	
					____ per ____	
					____ per ____	
					____ per ____	
					____ per ____	

© 2006 by PRO-ED, Inc.

Observation Record

Behavior Comparison

BIP-3

Student A: _____

Student B: _____

Date: _____

Class/Time: _____

Code: + if behavior is observed and − if it is not observed

Behavior: _____

TIME	STUDENT A	STUDENT B	NOTES/DESCRIPTION OF ACTIVITIES

© 2006 by PRO-ED, Inc.

Observation Record
Behavior Tracker

BIP–3

Name: _____

Behavior: _____

TOTAL
10
9
8
7
6
5
4
3
2
1

Date _____

TOTAL
10
9
8
7
6
5
4
3
2
1

Date _____

TOTAL
10
9
8
7
6
5
4
3
2
1

Date _____

TOTAL
10
9
8
7
6
5
4
3
2
1

Date _____

TOTAL
10
9
8
7
6
5
4
3
2
1

Date _____

Observation Record

Behavior Purpose

BIP-3

Name: _____ Date: _____

TIME/SETTING	OBSERVER	DESCRIPTION OF BEHAVIOR	PURPOSE OF BEHAVIOR					COMMENTS
			Avoidance/Escape	Attention	Self-Control Issue	Sensory/Emotional Reaction	Other	

© 2006 by PRO-ED, Inc.

BIP-3 | 55

Parent Information Record

Parent Contact

BIP-3

Student: _____

Parent Contact Information

	Mother	**Father**
Name:	_____	_____
Address:	_____	_____
	_____	_____
Telephone		
Home:	_____	_____
Work:	_____	_____
E-Mail:	_____	_____
Fax:	_____	_____

Date of Contact: _____

Person Initiating Contact: _____ Relationship to Student: _____

Type of Contact: ❏ Telephone   ❏ Fax

❏ E-Mail   ❏ Metting at School

❏ Meeting at Student's Home   ❏ Other _____

Purpose of Contact: _____

Brief Summary of Contact: _____

_____

_____

Follow-Up Agreed to: ❏ Yes   ❏ No

Timeline and Type of Follow-Up: _____

_____

Other Information: _____

_____

_____

Behavioral Intervention Planning–Third Edition

BIP-3

Functional Behavioral Assessment (FBA) Home Version

Student's Name: _____

Prioritized Behavior # _____ _____

Antecedents (Events or conditions occurring before or triggering the behavior)	**Behavior** (Exactly what the child does or does not do)	**Consequences** (Actions or events occurring after the behavior)	**Function of Behavior** (Hypothesized purpose of the behavior)

☐ Location in home: _____
 	
 ☐ Day of week or time of day: _____
 	
 ☐ Transition from: _____ to _____
 	
 ☐ Interruption in routine: _____
 	
 ☐ Directive or request to: _____
 	
 ☐ Consequences imposed: _____
 	
 ☐ Difficulty or frustration: _____
 	
 ☐ Person(s) in environment: _____
 	
 ☐ Other(s): _____ _____
	Behavior in observable, measurable terms: _____ _____ _____
	
	 Baseline measures of behavior
	 Frequency of behavior: _____
	 _____ per _____
	
	 Duration of behavior: _____
	 _____ per incident
	
	 Intensity of behavior: _____ _____ _____ _____
		☐ Behavior is ignored
		   ☐ On purpose
		   ☐ Incidentally
		
		 ☐ Adult attention
		   ☐ Reminder(s)
		   ☐ Repeated directive or request
		   ☐ Reprimand or warning
		
		 ☐ Attention from siblings or peers
		
		 ☐ Withdrawal or removal of directive or request
		
		 ☐ Loss of privilege: _____
		
		 ☐ Time-out (explain): _____
		
		 ☐ Other reductive consequence: _____
		
		 ☐ Other(s): _____ _____
			☐ Avoidance or escape
			   ☐ Avoid a directive or a request to: _____
			
			 ☐ Avoid a task or chore: _____
			
			 ☐ Avoid an activity: _____
			
			 ☐ Avoid person(s): _____
			
			 ☐ Gain attention
			   ☐ From parent
			   ☐ From siblings or peers
			
			 ☐ Sensory or emotional reaction due to
			   ☐ Fear or anxiety
			   ☐ Sensory relief or stimulation
			   ☐ Other: _____
			
			 ☐ Self-control issue related to
			   ☐ Frustration
			   ☐ Anger
			   ☐ Vengeance
			   ☐ Power or control
			   ☐ Intimidation
			
			 ☐ Other(s): _____ _____

© 2006 by PRO-ED, Inc.

Behavioral Intervention Planning–Third Edition

BIP-3

Functional Behavioral Assessment (FBA) Community Version

Student's Name: _____

Prioritized Behavior # _____ _____

Antecedents (Events or conditions occurring before or triggering the behavior)	**Behavior** (Exactly what the child does or does not do)	**Consequences** (Actions or events occurring after the behavior)	**Function of Behavior** (Hypothesized purpose of the behavior)
☐ Location in community or specific setting: _____ _____ ☐ Day of week or time of day: _____ ☐ Transition from: _____ to _____ ☐ Interruption in routine: _____ ☐ Directive or request to: _____ ☐ Consequences imposed: _____ ☐ Difficulty or frustration: _____ ☐ Person(s) in environment: _____ ☐ Other(s): _____ _____	Behavior in observable, measurable terms: _____ _____ _____ **Baseline measures of behavior** Frequency of behavior: _____ _____ per _____ Duration of behavior: _____ _____ per incident Intensity of behavior: _____ _____ _____	☐ Behavior is ignored ☐ On purpose ☐ Incidentally ☐ Adult attention ☐ Reminder(s) ☐ Repeated directive or request ☐ Reprimand or warning ☐ Attention from other significant person (indicate): _____ ☐ Withdrawal or removal of directive or request ☐ Loss of privilege: _____ ☐ Time out (explain): _____ ☐ Other reductive consequence: _____ ☐ Other(s): _____ _____	☐ Avoidance or escape ☐ Avoid a directive or a request to: _____ ☐ Avoid a task: _____ ☐ Avoid an activity: _____ ☐ Avoid person(s): _____ ☐ Gain attention ☐ From parent ☐ From significant person: _____ ☐ Sensory or emotional reaction due to ☐ Fear or anxiety ☐ Sensory relief or stimulation ☐ Other: _____ ☐ Self-control issue related to ☐ Frustration ☐ Anger ☐ Vengeance ☐ Power or control ☐ Intimidation ☐ Social situation ☐ Other(s): _____ _____

© 2006 by PRO-ED, Inc.

Administrative Resources

APPENDIX E

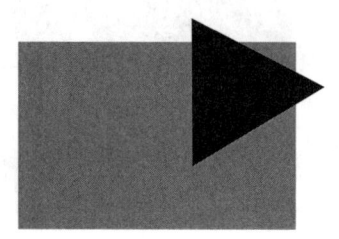

Discussion Guide: Series of Removals That Constitute a Pattern

When determining whether a series of removals constitutes a pattern, the IEP team may discuss these and other related questions.

1. How many times has the student been removed from his or her educational placement during the current school year?

2. For how long was each removal?

3. What is the total number of days that the student has been removed during the current school year?

4. What are the dates of the removals, and how many school days were there between each removal?

5. What were the behavioral incidents that lead to the removals?

6. How would you categorize the incidents (e.g., level of intensity or type)?

7. Were the behavioral incidents similar to each other? If so, how?

8. Were the behavioral incidents determined to have been a manifestation of the child's disability?

9. Is there other information to consider? If so, what?

Note. Section 300.536 explains the criteria for a change of placement under §§ 300.530 through 300.535. However, at the publication date of this manual, the final regulations for the IDEA 2004 reauthorization were not written. *Consult the final regulations when they are available, as this section may change.*

Behavioral Intervention Planning–Third Edition

B

Removal Record

Removal Record for _____ to _____ School Year

Name of Student: _____   Student's Disability: _____

Parent(s): _____   _____

Student's Teacher or Team Leader: _____

Date Removal Began and Ended	Length of Removal (Number of School Days)	Type of Removal (IAES[1], Another Setting, Suspension)	Number of School Days Since Last Removal	Incident or Type of Infraction Precipitating Removal
_____ _____	_____ days	_____	_____ days	_____
_____ _____	_____ days	_____	_____ days	_____
_____ _____	_____ days	_____	_____ days	_____
_____ _____	_____ days	_____	_____ days	_____
_____ _____	_____ days	_____	_____ days	_____
_____ _____	_____ days	_____	_____ days	_____
_____ _____	_____ days	_____	_____ days	_____
_____ _____	_____ days	_____	_____ days	_____
_____ _____	_____ days	_____	_____ days	_____
_____ _____	_____ days	_____	_____ days	_____
_____ _____	_____ days	_____	_____ days	_____

[1] IAES = Interim Alternative Educational Setting

© 2006 by PRO-ED, Inc.

Behavioral Intervention Planning–Third Edition — BIP-3

Manifestation Determination Flowchart

If the student has violated the student code of conduct, school personnel may consider unique circumstances for this specific student when deciding whether to order a change in placement.

Is a placement change to an IAES, another setting, or suspension for **NOT MORE than 10 school days** being considered?

YES ↓

If this alternative is applied to other students without disabilities for the same violation, then the student may be removed and **no Manifestation Determination is needed.**

Is a placement change to an IAES, another setting, or suspension for **MORE than 10 school days** being considered?

Is a placement change to an IAES, another setting, or suspension that is part of a **series of removals totaling more than 10 school days and constituting a pattern** being considered?

(See page 60 for an explanation of a series of removals constituting a pattern.)

YES ↓

Conduct a Manifestation Determination

If the decision is made to remove the student for more than 10 school days, within 10 school days of that decision the school district, parents, and relevant IEP team members shall review all relevant information, including the following:

- The IEP
- Teacher observations
- Relevant information provided by parents

The purpose of the review is to determine if either of the following instances applies. If *either* of these two applies, the behavior is a manifestation of the disability.

1. The conduct was *caused by, or had a direct and substantial relationship to* the student's disability.
2. The conduct was a *direct result of the Local Education Agency's (school district's) failure to implement the IEP.*

Is the behavior a manifestation of the disability? (See the next page.)

Is the behavior a manifestation of the disability?

YES ⇩

If the behavior is a manifestation of the disability, the student must

1. continue to receive educational services enabling progress toward IEP goals and participation in the general education curriculum; and,
2. if appropriate, receive
   - a functional behavioral assessment (FBA), and
   - behavioral intervention services and modifications (BIP and modifications).

In addition, the IEP team shall

1. conduct a functional behavioral assessment, if there is not one in place;
2. implement a BIP or review a previous plan for modification; and
3. return the student to his or her previous placement, unless parents and school district agree to a change in placement as part of a modified BIP or if the violation involved weapons, drugs, or infliction of serious bodily injury. *

NO ⇩

If the behavior is not a manifestation of the disability, you may apply the same disciplinary action applicable to students without disabilities, in the same manner, and for the same duration. This *does* include placement to an IAES.

The student must

1. continue to receive educational services enabling progress toward IEP goals and participation in the general education curriculum; and,
2. if appropriate, receive
   - a functional behavioral assessment (FBA), and
   - behavioral intervention services and modifications (BIP and modifications).

---

* Either the parents or the school district may request an appeal. During appeal, the student remains in the IAES pending a decision or until expiration of the time period allowed for students without disabilities, whichever occurs first, unless parents and the school district agree otherwise.

© 2006 by PRO-ED, Inc.

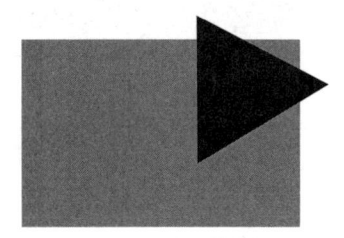

Administrator's Summary of Behavioral Intervention Plan (BIP)

Identifying Information

Name of Student: _____

Student's Disability: _____

Grade: _____ BIP Date: _____

Teacher/Case Manager: _____

Specific Behavioral Objectives

1. _____
2. _____
3. _____
4. _____

Indicate interventions by checking appropriate boxes.

A. Positive Environmental Supports
- ❏ Remove distracting materials
- ❏ Provide quiet, separate seating area
- ❏ Modify academic requirements
- ❏ Use visual cues, signals, or advance organizers
- ❏ Provide written or visual schedule
- ❏ Use proximity cues
- ❏ Provide choices related to assignments
- ❏ Use gestures, physical cues
- ❏ Minimize transition time
- ❏ Structure group supports
- ❏ Other: _____

B. Instructional Strategies
- ❏ Teach class rules and establish expectations, set limits
- ❏ Model desirable behavior
- ❏ Use strategic placement
- ❏ Role-play
- ❏ Coach through use of corrective feedback
- ❏ Provide literature-based lessons
- ❏ Monitor and provide written feedback
- ❏ Develop student–teacher contract
- ❏ Develop student–parent contract
- ❏ Teach self-monitoring
- ❏ Show and discuss videotapes
- ❏ Use team-building activities
- ❏ Provide social skills games
- ❏ Organize group discussions
- ❏ Other: _____

C. Positive Reinforcement
- ❏ Use frequent, consistent, specific verbal praise
- ❏ Provide positive social reinforcement
- ❏ Establish point system
- ❏ Establish in-class or in-school reward system
- ❏ Establish home–school reward system
- ❏ Establish token economy
- ❏ Provide consumable reinforcement
- ❏ Provide tangible reinforcement
- ❏ Refer to other adults for praise
- ❏ Use privileges or responsibilities
- ❏ Use private praise
- ❏ Use random drawings
- ❏ Other: _____

D. Reductive Consequences
- ❏ Use nonverbal signals
- ❏ Provide verbal reminder or reprimand
- ❏ Set up system of planned ignoring
- ❏ Use a structured warning system
- ❏ Assign essays and writing assignments
- ❏ Use cost-response procedures
- ❏ Provide time to cool off at desk or other area
- ❏ Implement loss of privileges
- ❏ Arrange student–teacher conference
- ❏ Implement previously agreed behavior contract
- ❏ Refer to counselor or mentor
- ❏ Telephone parent(s)
- ❏ Administrative consequences:
_____
_____
_____
_____

Assessment and Instructional Resources

APPENDIX F

Assessment Instruments

AGS Publishing
4201 Woodland Road
Circle Pines, MN 55014-1796
800/328-2560 • www.agsnet.com

Behavior Assessment System for Children–Second Edition (BASC–2)
Cecil R. Reynolds and Randy W. Kamphaus

BASC–2 provides the most comprehensive set of rating scales for children ages 2-0 through 21-11. These scales measure areas important for both IDEA and DSM–IV classifications. In addition, BASC–2 is respected for its developmental sensitivity. Best of all, you receive the most extensive view of adaptive and maladaptive behavior. BASC–2 applies a triangulation method for gathering information. By analyzing the child's behavior from three perspectives—Self, Teacher, and Parent—you get a more complete and balanced picture. Combined, these BASC–2 tools provide one of the most comprehensive systems currently available.

Hawthorne Educational Services, Inc.
800 Gray Oak Drive
Columbia, MO 65201
800/542-1673 • www.hes-inc.com

Behavior Disorders Identification Scale–Second Edition (BDIS–2)
Stephen B. McCarney and Tamara J. Arthaud

The BDIS–2 includes both a school and home version to provide an ecological perception of student behavior problems. The scale relies on direct behavioral observations by educators and parents or guardians. The BDIS–2 was designed to meet all state and federal guidelines for the identification of behaviorally disordered or emotionally disturbed students from 5 to 18 years of age. As a comprehensive evaluation instrument, the BDIS–2 progresses from assessment to program development to intervention.

Emotional or Behavior Disorder Scale–Revised (EBDS–R)
Stephen B. McCarney and Tamara J. Arthaud

The EBDS–R was developed to contribute to the early identification and service delivery for students with emotional or behavioral disorders. It is based on the National Mental Health and Special Education Coalition definition of emotional or behavioral disorder and the theoretical construct of the federal definition (IDEA). The Behavioral Component assesses three areas identified in the definition: Academic Progress, Social Relationships, and Personal Adjustment. The Vocational Component assesses the fourth area identified in the definition: Work Related, Interpersonal Relations, and Social/Community Expectations.

PRO-ED, Inc.
8700 Shoal Creek Boulevard
Austin, TX 78757-6897
800/897-3202 • www.proedinc.com

Behavioral and Emotional Rating Scale–Second Edition (BERS–2)
Michael H. Epstein and Jennifer M. Sharma

Designed for use in schools, mental health clinics, and child welfare agencies, the BERS–2 helps to measure the personal strengths of children ages 5-0 through 18-11. The BERS–2 contains 52 items that measure five aspects of a child's strength: interpersonal strength, involvement with family, intrapersonal strength, school functioning, and affective strength. The scale can be completed in approximately 10 minutes by teachers, parents, counselors, or other persons knowledgeable about the child. The BERS provides an overall strength score and five subtest scores. Information from the BERS is useful in evaluating children for prereferral services and in placing children for specialized services.

Behavior Rating Profile–Second Edition (BRP–2)
Linda Brown and Donald D. Hammill

The BRP–2 is a unique battery of six norm-referenced instruments that provides different evaluations of a student's behavior at home, at school, and in interpersonal relationships from the varied perspectives of parents, teachers, peers, and the target students themselves. The responses allow examiners to test different diagnostic hypotheses when confronted with reports of problem behavior. The BRP–2 can identify students whose behavior is perceived to be deviant, the settings in which behavior problems are prominent, and the persons whose perceptions of a student's behavior are different from those of other respondents. The BRP–2 is appropriate for students in Grades 1 through 12.

Preschool and Kindergarten Behavior Scales–Second Edition (PKBS–2)
Kenneth W. Merrell

The PKBS–2 is a standardized behavior rating scale designed for use with children ages 3 through 6 years. This unique behavior rating scale is easy to use, very practical, and based on a solid foundation of research. With 76 items on two separate scales, it provides an integrated and functional appraisal of the social skills and problem behaviors of young children. The scales can be completed by a variety of behavioral informants, such as parents, teachers, and other caregivers.

The Social Skills scale includes 34 items on three subscales: Social Cooperation, Social Interaction, and Social Independence. The Problem Behavior scale includes 42 items on two subscales: Externalizing Problems and Internalizing Problems. In addition, five supplementary problem behavior subscales are available for optional use.

Scale for Assessing Emotional Disturbance (SAED)
Michael H. Epstein and Douglas Cullinan

This standardized, norm-referenced scale will help you identify children and adolescents who qualify for the federal special education category, Emotional Disturbance. SAED is based on the federal terminology and definition of serious emotional disturbance, as presented in the Individuals with Disabilities Education Act of 1990 (IDEA). The scale can be completed in less than 10 minutes by teachers, counselors, parents, and other individuals familiar with the child. Information from the SAED is useful in understanding the emotional and behavioral disorders of children, identifying students who may meet the criteria for the serious emotional disturbance education disability category, selecting appropriate education goals for an IEP, and periodically evaluating student progress toward desired outcomes.

Social–Emotional Dimension Scale–Second Edition (SEDS–2)
Jerry B. Hutton and Timothy G. Roberts

SEDS–2 is a rating scale for teachers, counselors, and psychologists to screen students age 5-6 through 18-6 who are at risk for conduct disorders, behavior problems, or emotional disturbance. It assesses physical or fear reaction, depressive reaction, avoidance of peer interaction, avoidance of teacher interaction, aggressive interaction, and inappropriate behaviors. Normed on a nationwide representative sample of students, it provides percentiles for the six targeted areas as well as a Total Behavior Score (percentile), a Behavior Quotient (BQ), and a Behavior Observation Web (BOW) that plots student performance graphically.

Sopris West
P.O. Box 1809
Longmont, CO 80502-1802
800/547-6747 • www.sopriswest.com

Systematic Screening for Behavior Disorders (SSBD)
Hill M. Walker and Herbert H. Severson

SSBD is a cost-effective process for the systematic screening and identification of K–6 students who may be at risk for developing behavior disorders. The SSBD screening process is proactive, and incorporates a three-stage, multigated process. It takes into consideration teacher judgments and direct observation. The kit contains three manuals, a videotape, an audiotape, and forms.

Instructional Resources

AAMR
444 North Capitol Street, NW
Suite 846
Washington, DC 20001-1512
800/424-3688 • www.aamr.org

Designing Positive Behavior Support Plans
Linda Bambara and Tim Knoster

This book provides a conceptual framework for understanding, designing, and evaluating positive behavior support plans. It begins with a functional assessment to identify environmental influences and individual strengths and interests. Behavior support plans are then customized to include multiple support strategies that emphasize alternative skill training, environmental adaptations, and lifestyle enhancements.

Attainment Company, Inc.
504 Commerce Parkway
P.O. Box 930160
Verona, WI 53593-0160
800/327-4269 • www.attainmentcompany.com

Why Johnny Doesn't Behave
Barbara Bateman and Annemieke Golly

The authors focus on 20 concrete "tips" to help you avoid behavioral problems, including making clear classroom expectations, directly teaching expectations, minimizing attention for minor inappropriate behaviors and paying attention to behavior you want to encourage. The second section is dedicated to Functional Behavior Assessments and Behavioral Intervention Plans, beginning with an explanation of each and ending with sample FBAs and BIPs so you can learn how to write your own.

Brookes Publishing
P.O. Box 10624
Baltimore, MD 21285-0624
800/638-3775 • www.brookespublishing.com

Behavioral Support
Rachel Janney and Martha E. Snell

Educators face the challenge of managing classroom behavior, teaching acceptable social skills, and maintaining curriculum standards in diverse classroom settings. In this easy-to-read manual, general and special education teachers, counselors, related services staff, and family members will gain insight into students' behaviors and discover fresh, proactive ideas on how to help students develop appropriate behavioral skills. A quick and concise guide to current research and recommended methods, *Behavioral Support* provides the field-tested strategies professionals need for working with students with disabilities.

Brooks/Cole
Thomson Learning
P.O. Box 6904
Florence, KY 41022-6904
800/354-9706 • www.brookscole.com

Functional Assessment and Program Development for Problem Behavior–Second Edition
Robert E. O'Neill, Robert H. Horne, Richard W. Albin, Keith Storey, and Jeffrey R. Sprague

This guide to functional assessment procedures includes a variety of strategies for assessing problem behavior situations and presents a systematic approach for designing behavioral support programs based on those assessments. Professionals and students alike will appreciate the way the authors help readers learn to conduct functional assessments and develop their own intervention programs.

The Council for Exceptional Children (CEC)
P.O. Box 79026, Dept. K6092
Baltimore, MD 21279-0026
800/232-7323 • www.cec.sped.org

Back Off, Cool Down, Try Again
Sylvia Rockwell

This book describes how to work with groups of students with behavioral or emotional problems using the stages of group development as the basis for classroom management. Presents strategies for documentation and consultation, and provides reproducible behavior management forms and instructional planning forms.

Good Talking Words
Lucy Hart Paulson and Richard A. van den Pol

These fun activities and materials help you teach communication skills, problem-solving skills, and language. The program includes a 96-page manual filled with lesson outlines and storybook title suggestions; 43 blackline masters of reproducible certificates, coupons, and coloring pages to reinforce appropriate behavior and make learning fun;

11 colorful posters that encourage students to recall and use their newly acquired skills; and 19 Skill Pictures that demonstrate each behavior.

Free Spirit Publishing
400 First Avenue North, Suite 616
Minneapolis, MN 55401-1724
800/735-7323 • www.freespirit.com

Teaching Kids with Learning Difficulties in the Regular Classroom
Susan Winebrenner

This book is a gold mine of proven, practical ways to help students labeled "special education," "slow," "remedial," or "LD" succeed in the general education classroom—without remediating, watering down content, lowering expectations, or depriving other students of the time and attention they need. Includes 52 reproducible handouts.

Guilford Press
72 Spring Street
New York, NY 10012
800/365-7006 • www.guilford.com

Conducting School-Based Functional Behavioral Assessments
T. Steuart Watson and Mark W. Steege

This manual takes school practitioners step by step through conducting functional behavioral assessments and then using those assessments to plan effective interventions. The authors present a cogent rationale for the use of Functional Behavioral Assessment, clearly explaining its advantages over traditional approaches to dealing with problem behaviors. All of the tools needed to complete a reliable and valid FBA are provided, including reproducible forms, questionnaires, and worksheets.

Effective School Interventions
Natalie Rathvon

This practical book presents more than 70 interventions that have been empirically demonstrated to improve the classroom learning environment, bolster academic achievement, and enhance student behavior and social competence. Each intervention is delineated in a brief, standardized format that describes its purpose, lists needed materials, and provides step-by-step implementation procedures. All of the interventions can easily be delivered by general classroom teachers and make use of existing or readily available resources.

Skills Training for Children with Behavior Problems–Revised Edition
Michael L. Bloomquist

Grounded in the latest developmental knowledge and best practices, this popular guide addresses a broad array of behavior and adjustment difficulties. A wealth of practical tools are provided to build self-control in struggling children and teens; get social, emotional, and academic development back on track; and reduce family stress. Including over 25 reproducible tools in a large-size format, the book can be used by parents on their own or in collaboration with practitioners in clinic, school, or community settings.

Hawthorne Educational Services, Inc.
800 Gray Oak Drive
Columbia, MO 65201
800/542-1673 • www.hes-inc.com

The Pre-Referral Intervention Manual
Stephen B. McCarney

States are mandating prereferral intervention activities, and this manual provides a direct response to the mandate. It may be used by a teacher or group of educators to develop a comprehensive plan of intervention strategies for the student. The manual contains intervention strategies for the 219 most common learning and behavior problems and includes an appendix of materials for the implementation of the behavioral interventions.

The Teacher's Guide to Behavioral Interventions
Kathy Cummins Wunderlich

The most comprehensive reference of its kind today (291 pages). The guide includes proven intervention strategies for the most common behavior problems found in schools and hundreds of goals and objectives for developing an IEP for the student who is identified for special education services.

Jossey-Bass
10475 Crosspoint Boulevard
Indianapolis, IN 46256
877/762-2974 • www.josseybass.com/WileyCDA

Special Kids Problem Solver
Kenneth Shore

Written by an experienced school psychologist, this unique resource gives classroom teachers and specialists at all levels the key information and practical strategies they need to recognize and respond effectively to 30 of the most common problems encountered in today's classrooms, including academic problems, behavioral problems, and physical problems.

Love Publishing Company
9101 East Kenyon Avenue
Suite 2200
Denver, CO 80237
303/221-7333 • www.lovepublishing.com

Functional Behavioral Assessment
Mary E. McConnell

This book is designed specifically for persons who have limited training in applied behavior analysis and functional assessment procedures. This easy-to-use manual will help educators understand the purpose and meaning of the functional behavior assessment process and how to identify and assess behavior. It shows how to develop and write effective Behavior Intervention Plans using data collected during the functional assessment.

Teaching Social–Emotional Skills at School and Home
Linda K. Elksnin and Nick Elksnin

This book is designed to provide teachers and parents with strategies for teaching children and youth to become socially and emotionally competent. It is research-based yet practical and easy to read. The authors examine all aspects of social–emotional learning, including emotional literacy, social problem solving, and the social skills essential for making friends and succeeding in school. Assessment approaches; practical activities; real-life vignettes; and numerous forms, checklists, and planning sheets are included.

Prentice Hall
One Lake Street
Upper Saddle River, NJ 07458
800/922-0579 • www.pearsoned.com

Functional Assessment–Second Edition
Lynette K. Chandler and Carol Dahlquist

This text is unique in its wide application to a number of settings. The comprehensive, practical treatment of functional assessment addresses preschool through high school levels, general education and self-contained classroom settings, and special and general education student populations. Its strong use of vignettes and open-ended case studies promotes problem solving among readers as they identify the function of behavior, choose intervention options, and pinpoint typical functional assessment practices.

Understanding the Purpose of Challenging Behavior
James Artesani

This brief handbook is most appropriate as a supplement for courses in special education assessment, behavior disorders and behavior management. It defines functional assessment, describes when it is most useful how it is related to the IDEA, and finally offers methods for conducting functional assessments.

PRO-ED, Inc.
8700 Shoal Creek Boulevard
Austin, TX 78757-6897
800/897-3202 • www.proedinc.com

Beyond Behavior Modification–Third Edition
Joseph S. Kaplan with Jane Carter

Much of the material in this popular text has been rewritten since the first edition. A new introductory chapter includes preventive behavior-management strategies and a comparison of popular approaches to behavior management. The extensive coverage of data collection is expanded to include new material on trend estimation and interpretation. The first half of the book focuses on traditional behavior modification, and the second half presents a social learning theory approach. Short assessments called "checkpoints" are embedded within each chapter in addition to the more comprehensive end-of-chapter assessments, allowing the reader to test his or her understanding of the material as he or she reads it. Concrete examples are used throughout.

Beyond Functional Assessment
Joseph S. Kaplan

Beyond Functional Assessment provides all of the prerequisites and assessments a teacher, school psychologist, or behavioral cosultant needs to evaluate troublesome student behaviors including, but not limited to, noncompliance, physical or verbal aggression (with or without provocation), destruction of property, disruption for attention, and refusal to work. Based on the social–cognitive model, the assessments focus on cognitions and emotions in addition to those environmental variables that contribute to maladaptive behavior in children and youth. Assessment results lead directly to behavioral intervention plans including performance objectives.

Conflict in the Classroom–Fifth Edition
Nicholas J. Long, William Morse, and Ruth G. Newman

The fifth edition of *Conflict in the Classroom* continues the psychoeducational fusion between sound mental health and educational practices in the classroom. The authors have confronted the four complex problems facing educators today: (a) what to do with the increasing number of already troubled and seriously at-risk students in our schools; (b) how to help the growing number of students who are struggling with fearsome family and community conditions and are on the brink of failing life and school; (c) how to develop accountable programs that do the right things and get the desired results; and (d) what psychoeducational skills to use as the wall between general and special education is breached, and all teachers become special education teachers.

Coping with Noncompliance in the Classroom
Hill M. Walker and Janet Eaton Walker

This booklet enhances classroom teachers' understanding of student noncompliance and provides a variety of guidelines, strategies, and recommendations for coping effectively with the occurrence of noncompliance. Specific intervention strategies are described, and application guidelines are illustrated through a series of case studies. The material presents a positive approach to fostering student compliance and for dealing with noncompliance episodes when they occur.

Creating a High-Interest Classroom
Elaine Young

Visionary instructors are able to view, inspire, and guide one student at a time while facilitating high-performing teams of cooperative learners who in turn nourish one another's enthusiasm, competence, and growth. This book shows you how to nourish and inspire all of your students and bring out the best each has to offer. You will learn how to discover the true interests of individual students and translate those interests into a unified, intrinsically exciting curriculum. With concrete classroom experiences; easy-to-implement activities; and practical, step-by-step guidelines, the book describes how to open doors to growth and discovery, how to help students learn more about their world and themselves and how to fill students with joy and enthusiasm about the notion of learning.

Handbook of Individual Strategies for Classroom Discipline
W. George Selig and Alan A. Arroyo

This handbook contains a complete repertoire of discipline strategies for the classroom teacher or school psychologist. Organized for quick reference, this handbook lets you look up a specific classroom problem and choose—from an array of options—a discipline strategy that is not only appropriate for the problem but also compatible with the particular student's behavior style and level of motivation.

How To Improve Classroom Behavior Series
Saul Axelrod and Steven C. Mathews

This series is unique in that each book describes a particular problem and then provides teachers with specific, easy-to-apply steps that can be used to modify problem behaviors constructively. The format of the books is easy to read and interactive. After reading each book, teachers will have a good idea of how to solve common classroom problems and create an atmosphere that is productive and conducive to learning. The following is a list of titles in the series:
- How To Help Students Remain Seated
- How To Deal Effectively with Lying, Stealing, and Cheating
- How To Prevent and Safely Manage Physical Aggression and Property Destruction
- How To Help Students Play and Work Together
- How To Deal with Students Who Challenge and Defy Authority
- How To Deal Effectively with Whining and Tantrum Behaviors
- How To Help Students Follow Directions, Pay Attention, and Stay On-Task
- How To Deal Effectively with Inappropriate Talking and Noisemaking

How To Manage Behavior Series
Series Editors: R. Vance Hall and Marilyn L. Hall

These nontechnical, step-by-step instructional manuals define each procedure, provide numerous examples, and allow the reader to make oral or written responses. These short but informative manuals can be used to teach practitioners and parents specific behavioral procedures for managing the behavior of children, students, or other persons whose

behavior may be creating a disruption or interference. The following is a list of titles in the series:
- *How To Use Planned Ignoring (Extinction)–Second Edition*
- *How To Negotiate a Behavioral Contract–Second Edition*
- *How To Select Reinforcers–Second Edition*
- *How To Use Systematic Attention and Approval–Second Edition*
- *How To Use Time Out–Second Edition*
- *How To Use Positive Practice, Self-Correction, and Overcorrection–Second Edition*
- *How To Use Token Economy and Point Systems–Second Edition*
- *How To Maintain Behavior–Second Edition*
- *How To Teach Through Modeling and Imitation–Second Edition*
- *How To Motivate Others Through Feedback–Second Edition*
- *How To Use Group Contingencies*
- *How To Teach Social Skills*
- *How To Use Prompts To Initiate Behavior*
- *How To Teach Self-Control Through Trigger Analysis*

I Can Behave
Darlene S. Mannix

I Can Behave revolves around an illustrated storybook comprising 10 stories and 125 full-page drawings. Each of the 10 stories focuses on a specific classroom dilemma ("My Turn, Your Turn"—letting others talk; "Marvin and His Mouth"—using a quiet voice). Lessons include Working Independently, Waiting for Help, Doing Careful Work, Handling Classroom Frustrations, and Sitting Still. The curriculum is appropriate for general or special education classes. The revised format offers the complete program in one manual, which includes blackline masters for the teacher's unlimited use in the classroom.

Life Space Crisis Intervention–Second Edition
Nicholas J. Long, Mary M. Wood, and Frank A. Fecser

Here is a professional resource for educators, psychologists, and counselors that focuses on Life Space Crisis Intervention, a strategy to help guide young people through stressful experiences. The second edition of this important book offers a significant breakthrough in teaching professionals the unique skills of interviewing children and youth during interpersonal crises. Part One prepares an adult to deal with all aspects of student stress. Part Two teaches the six sequential steps involved in carrying out successful life space crisis intervention, based on Fritz Redl's concepts. Part Three describes six types of therapeutic life space crisis interventions that are typical and beneficial to students in conflict.

Managing Passive-Aggressive Behavior of Children and Youth at School and Home: The Angry Smile
Nicholas J. Long and Jody E. Long

The angry smile is the first comprehensive, insightful, and realistic description of the passive-aggressive student at school and home. Passive-aggressive behavior is as pervasive as the air around us, yet it is not usually recognized until it pollutes our mental health. Passive aggression is potentially more destructive to interpersonal relationships than aggressive behavior. Aggression is overt and painful, but passive aggression is covert, insidious, and can last a lifetime. This is a breakthrough book for all parents, teachers, and counselors who have to live, teach, and survive with a passive–aggressive student.

Outrageous Behavior Mod
Barry T. Christian

This handbook is for educators who have studied behavior management theory but have not had success in managing difficult students. Many of the methods presented are powerfully hypnotic and strategic in nature and are intended to effectively neutralize student resistance at a deeper personality level. The handbook is not at all about points and charts, time-outs, or happy stickers. These methods were developed specifically for those hard-core "you can't make me" students and actually use student resistance to fuel compliance.

Personal Power
Ruth Herman Wells

The *Personal Power* series is the nation's only comprehensive system to rapidly and effectively teach problem youth to succeed in school. This series was designed to turn around aggressive, withdrawn, unmotivated, absent, learning disabled, and uncontrollable youth in Grades 4 through 12. The series was developed to give teachers, counselors, psychologists, foster parents, and youth professionals the tools needed to teach youth how to succeed in school, emotionally and socially. The series includes volumes focusing on three areas of success—in school, with oneself, and with others. Lessons include cartoons, contests, games, experiments, stories, role-plays, and other innovative devices.

Practical Charts for Managing Behavior
Lynn Lavelle

Take the hassle out of documenting your students' social-skill progress with this revolutionary collection of charts. Choose from 40 different extensively field-tested charts, each of which is uniquely designed to meet the needs of the observer and the behaviors of the person being monitored. If you enjoy designing or tailoring your own charts, you can use these effective designs as templates, but these are tools you can read, review, and use immediately. These charts will noticeably enhance the processes of observation; positive reinforcement; behavior management; and communication among staff, parents, and the student.

Practical Ideas That Really Work for Students with Disruptive, Defiant, or Difficult Behaviors
Kathleen McConnell, Gail Ryser, and James R. Patton

Each of the *Practical Ideas That Really Work for Students with Disruptive, Defiant, or Difficult Behaviors* includes two components:

1. an easy-to-use evaluation form to rate a student's behavior, select and plan for appropriate interventions, and document progress; and

2. a book of practical ideas, containing suggestions for interventions, explanations of strategies, reproducible forms, and helpful illustrations and examples.

The materials are organized into two age-appropriate versions. One is designed for students in Preschool through Grade 4 and emphasizes visual communication strategies ideal for young students. The other version, appropriate for Grade 5 through Grade 12 students, focuses on interventions specially designed to meet the unique needs of older students. The behaviors addressed are organized into four categories, each focusing on an area of problematic behavior commonly reported among school-age students. Both the behaviors and their corresponding interventions have been well researched to ensure identification of high-priority problems as well as maximally effective solutions. Other *Practical Ideas* materials are available for specific disabilities.

Preventing School Failure–Second Edition
Thomas C. Lovitt

In this second edition there are 134 tactics in 16 chapters; the 16 chapter titles are Attendance, Motivation, Study Skills, Basic Skills, Homework, Adapting Materials, Testing and Grading, Social Skills, Participation, Goals, Peer Mediated Instruction, Self-Esteen, Classroom Management, Self-Management, Health, and Parents. Each tactic is written in an identical format, which consists of five sections: Background, Who Can Benefit, Procedures, Modifications/Considerations, and Monitor. Teachers have found this design easy to read and to implement. The majority of tactics are based on research. They are all accompanied by traditional journal and textbook citations, and several come with Website references.

20 Lessons in Self-Control and Anger Management for Middle School Students
Gerry Dunne

Teach middle school students in small or large groups how to manage their own behavior with these dynamic activities. The best of the best, these lessons come right to the point. They teach the specific skills and strategies middle school students need to gain self control and manage their anger. This book may be used in conjunction with the *Anger and Conflict Management: Personal Handbook* for added emphasis.

The Waksman Social Skills Curriculum for Adolescents–Fourth Editin
Steven Waksman and Deborah Denney Waksman

This popular and effective curriculum is now redesigned for easier application. Enjoy the ease of using reproducible lessons to teach appropriate assertive behavior skills to adolescents with and without disabilities. You will find that the 9-week, 18-lesson format contains specific goals, objectives, worksheets, homework assignments, and instructions. The program is particularly helpful with children and adolescents ages 10 to 15 years who display social-skill deficits, behavior disorders, hyperactivity, and emotional problems.

The Walker Social Skills Curriculum

The ACCEPTS Program: A Curriculum for Children's Effective Peer and Teacher Skills
Hill M. Walker, Scott McConnell, Deborah Holmes, Bonnie Todis, Jackie Walker, and Nancy Golden

ACCEPTS is a complete curriculum for teaching classroom and peer-to-peer social skills to children with or without disabilities in Grades K through 6. The curriculum, designed for use by general and special education teachers, cognitively teaches social skills as subject-matter content. It can be taught in one-to-one, small-group, or large-group formats.

The ACCESS Program: Adolescent Curriculum for Communication and Effective Social Skills
Hill M. Walker, Bonnie Todis, Deborah Holmes, and Gary Horton

ACCESS is a complete curriculum for teaching effective social skills to students at middle school and high school levels. The program teaches peer-to-peer skills, skills for relating to adults, and self-management skills. Designed for use by both general and special education teachers, it may be taught in one-to-one, small-group, or large-group formats.

Research Press
P.O. Box 9177, Dept. 971
Champaign, IL 61826
800/519-2707 • www.researchpress.com

Break It Up
Arnold P. Goldstein, James Palumbo, Susan Striepling, and Anne Marie Voutsinas

This book offers step-by-step procedures for establishing a team approach to safely handle student disruptiveness and aggression. It includes a comprehensive fight management system based on reports of 1,000 episodes of student aggression and its management. The reports were submitted by teachers of all grade levels.

Connecting with Others
Rita C. Richardson and Elizabeth T. Evans

This program integrates a variety of strategies for teaching social and emotional competence to students in kindergarten through middle school. It is a fun, proactive program that helps students learn to be sensitive to differences, resolve conflicts without resorting to violence, and show understanding, tolerance, and acceptance of others. This is a flexible program that allows teachers to be creative and adjust lessons to the needs of their students. There are four volumes: Grades K–2, Grades 3–5, Grades 6–8, and Grades 9–12.

I Can Problem Solve
Myrna B. Shure

This program is both preventive and rehabilitative. It is effective in helping children learn to resolve interpersonal problems and prevent antisocial behaviors. ICPS teaches children how to think, not what to think. They learn that behavior has causes, that people have feelings, and that there is more than one way to solve a problem. Impulsive students become better able to share, cooperate, and get along with others. Inhibited students become more outgoing and better able to stand up for their rights. ICPS is available in separate volumes for three developmental levels: preschool, kindergarten and primary grades, and intermediate elementary grades.

The Prepare Curriculum
Arnold P. Goldstein

This program provides prosocial skills training for use with middle school and high school students—especially those who are chronically aggressive, withdrawn, or weak in prosocial competencies. The curriculum consists of a series of 10 course-length interventions. Training methods involve games, simulations, role plays, group discussions, and other activities that enhance group participation and motivation for learning.

Skillstreaming the Adolescent
Arnold P. Goldstein, Robert P. Sprafkin, N. Jane Gershaw, and Paul Klein

This valuable book presents a prosocial skills group training program for adolescents, especially those who display aggression, immaturity, withdrawal, or other problem behaviors. It is designed to help teens increase self-esteem and develop competence in dealing with peers, family, and authority figures. The training approach uses teacher modeling, student role-playing, performance feedback, and transfer training.

Skillstreaming the Elementary School Child
Ellen McGinnis and Arnold P. Goldstein

This widely used book provides a training program that addresses the prosocial skill needs of children, especially those who display aggression, immaturity, withdrawal, or other problem behaviors. Although the program is designed for use with small groups of students, it is often adapted for use with larger groups. The training approach uses teacher modeling, student role playing, performance feedback, and transfer training.

Thinking, Feeling, Behaving
Ann Vernon

This comprehensive and easy-to-use curriculum is based on the principles of Rational Emotive Therapy. It helps students learn to use positive mental health concepts in overcoming irrational beliefs, negative feelings and attitudes, and the negative consequences that may result. The curriculum consists of two separate volumes—one for children (Grades 1–6) and one for adolescents (Grades 7–12). Each volume contains 90 field-tested activities that have been carefully arranged by grade level.

Sopris West
P.O. Box 1809
Longmont, CO 80502-1802
800/547-6747 • www.sopriswest.com

The Acting-Out Child–Second Edition
Hill M. Walker

This extensively revised, expanded, and updated edition outlines procedures for effectively managing the behavior of children who act out in the school environment. This research-based material empowers general education teachers, special and resource classroom teachers, and other school professionals to understand and address more effectively the challenges that such children and youth present on a daily basis.

Behavior Intervention Planning
Terry M. Scott, Carl J. Liaupsin, and C. Michael Nelson

Here is a fresh approach to creating successful Behavior Intervention Plans. This interactive, easy-to-use instructional CD-ROM provides in-depth, logical information about the elements of a high-quality BIP. The six-step process includes
1. determining the function of the problem behavior,
2. selecting a replacement behavior,
3. designing a teaching plan,
4. arranging the environment to facilitate success,
5. developing consequences, and
6. writing behavior objectives.

The Teacher's Encyclopedia of Behavior Management
Randall S. Sprick and Lisa M. Howard

The Teacher's Encyclopedia of Behavior Management is a comprehensive resource for elementary and middle or junior high school teachers trying to improve student behavior and academic achievement. More than 100 specific problems are included—each listed alphabetically, cross-referenced to other behavior problems, and indexed so that the teacher can quickly find easy-to-implement interventions for just about any behavior or motivational problem likely to occur at school.

The Tough Kid Book
Ginger Rhode, William R. Jenson, and H. Kenton Reavis

This book provides techniques to address student aggression, noncompliance, and poor academic performance. It is a practical program that is not only effective but can be implemented quickly and inexpensively. The research-validated solutions included in this book help to reduce disruptive behavior in tough kids without big investments of the teacher's time, money, or emotions. These solutions also provide tough kids with behavioral, academic, and social survival skills.

Wadsworth
Thomson Learning
P.O. Box 6904
Florence, KY 41022-6904
800/354-9706 • www.wadsworth.com

Functional Analysis of Problem Behavior
Alan C. Repp and Robert H. Horner

This book contains several articles by experts in the fields of special education and psychology. Each article explores the issues, theories, and practices of assessing problem behavior and determining how to use this information. Together, the articles of this text present current advances in the use of functional assessment technology: taking the techniques and strategies of traditional functional analysis and using this information to construct clinical interventions. Three sections focus on the following topics: how functional assessment can be used to intervene effectively and change problem behavior, common procedures for using functional assessment in the preschool and school classroom, and new directions and trends in the field of functional assessment.

Journals

The Council for Exceptional Children (CEC)
P.O. Box 79026, Dept. K6092
Baltimore, MD 21279-0026
800/232-7323 • www.cec.sped.org

Teaching Exceptional Children

Teaching Exceptional Children (TEC) is a practical classroom-oriented magazine that explores instructional methods, materials, and techniques for working with children who have disabilities or who are gifted. Articles reflect approaches that blend theory with practice. TEC also brings its readers the latest data on technology, assistive technology, and procedures and techniques with applications to students with exceptionalities. The focus on its practical content is on immediate application. *Published six times a year.*

Behavioral Disorders

Behavioral Disorders (BD) is a publication of the Council for Children with Behavioral Disorders. BD publishes reports of research, program evaluations, and position papers related to the education of children and youth with emotional and behavioral disorders. *Published quarterly.*

Heldref Publications
1319 Eighteenth Street, NW
Washington, DC 20036-1802
800/365-9753 • www.heldref.org

Preventing School Failure

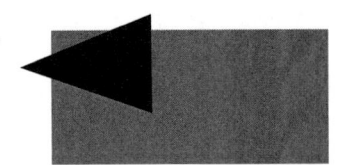

Preventing School Failure is the journal for educators and parents seeking strategies for promoting the success of students with learning and behavioral problems. It spotlights examples of programs and practices that are helping children. Practical and specific articles in preventing school failure are written by teachers, teacher educators, and parents. *Published quarterly.*

PRO-ED, Inc.
8700 Shoal Creek Boulevard
Austin, TX 78757-6897
800/897-3202 • www.proedinc.com

Journal of Emotional and Behavioral Disorders

The *Journal of Emotional and Behavioral Disorders* (JEBD) is an international, multidisciplinary journal featuring articles on research, practice, and commentary related to individuals with emotional and behavioral disorders. JEBD presents topics of interest to individuals representing a wide range of disciplines including corrections, psychiatry, mental health, counseling, rehabilitation, education, and psychology. *Published quarterly.*

Intervention in School and Clinic

Intervention in School and Clinic is one of the oldest and most widely read professional publications in special and remedial education. It is a practitioner-oriented journal designed to provide practical, research-based ideas to those who work with students with severe learning disabilities and emotional/behavioral problems for whom typical classroom instruction is not effective. Emphasis is placed on providing information that can be easily implemented in school or clinic settings. *Published five times a year.*

Journal of Positive Behavior Interventions

The *Journal of Positive Behavior Interventions* (JPBI) deals with principles of positive behavioral support in school, home, and community settings for people with challenges in behavioral adaptation. Features of JPBI include empirical research reports, commentaries, program descriptions, discussion of family supports, and coverage of timely issues. *Published quarterly.*

Remedial and Special Education

Remedial and Special Education (RASE) is a professional journal that bridges the gap between theory and practice. Emphasis is on topical reviews, syntheses of reasearch, field evaluation studies, and recommendations for the practice of remedial and special education. RASE offers articles that address issues involving the education of individuals for whom typical instruction is not effective and includes coverage of controversial topics, book reviews, commentaries, and editorials. *Published six times a year.*

APPENDIX G

Proposed Regulations

At the publication date of this manual, the final regulations for the IDEA 2004 reauthorization were not written. Consult the final regulations when they are available, as the sections provided in this appendix may change.

Section 300.324 (a) of the December 3, 2004 IDEA discusses the development of the IEP. A list of items that the team must discuss in developing each child's IEP is included.

§ 300.324   Development, review, and revision of IEP.

(a) Development of IEP. (1) *General.* In developing each child's IEP, the IEP Team must consider—
   (i) The strengths of the child;
   (ii) The concerns of the parents for enhancing the education of their child;
   (iii) The results of the initial or most recent evaluation of the child; and
   (iv) The academic, developmental, and functional needs of the child.

One part of that section specifically requires the team to consider the use of positive behavioral interventions and supports, and other strategies, to address the behavior of students whose behavior impedes their learning or that of others. This information, provided below, is the basis for the emphasis on positive strategies when developing a Behavioral Intervention Plan (BIP).

(2) *Consideration of special factors.* The IEP Team must—
   (i) In the case of a child whose behavior impedes the child's learning or that of others, consider the use of positive behavioral interventions and supports, and other strategies, to address that behavior;

The IDEA discussion of a change of placement because of disciplinary removals can be found in Sections 300.530 through 300.535. This includes information about definitions related to change of placement issues, determination of the setting, appeals, placement during appeals, protections for children not yet eligible for special education, and related services.

§ 300.530   Authority of school personnel.

(a) *Case-by-case determination.* School personnel may consider any unique circumstances on a case-by-case basis when determining whether a change in placement, consistent with the requirements of this section, is appropriate for a child with a disability who violates a code of student conduct.

(b) *General.* (1) School personnel under this section may remove a child with a disability who violates a code of student conduct from their current placement to an appropriate interim alternative educational setting, another setting, or suspension, for not more than 10 consecutive school days (to the extent those alternatives are applied to children without disabilities), and for additional removals of not more than 10 consecutive school days in that same school year for separate incidents of misconduct (as long as those removals do not constitute a change of placement under §300.536).

(2) After a child with a disability has been removed from his or her current placement for 10 school days in the same school year, during any subsequent days of removal the public agency must provide services to the extent required under paragraph (d) of this section.

(c) *Additional authority.* For disciplinary changes in placement that would exceed 10 consecutive school days, if the behavior that gave rise to the violation of the school code is determined not to be a manifestation of the child's disability pursuant to paragraph (e) of this section, school personnel may apply the relevant disciplinary procedures to children with disabilities in the same manner and for the same duration as the procedures would be applied to children without disabilities, except as provided in paragraph (d) of this section.

(d) *Services.* (1) Except as provided in paragraphs (d)(3) and (d)(4) of this section, a child with a disability who is removed from the child's current placement pursuant to paragraphs (b), (c), or (g) of this section must—

(i) Continue to receive educational services, so as to enable the child to continue to participate in the general education curriculum, although in another setting, and to progress toward meeting the goals set out in the child's IEP; and

(ii) Receive, as appropriate, a functional behavioral assessment, and behavioral intervention services and modifications, that are designed to address the behavior violation so that it does not recur.

(2) The services required by paragraph (d)(1) of this section may be provided in an interim alternative educational setting.

(3) A public agency need not provide services during periods of removal under paragraph (b) of this section to a child with a disability who has been removed from his or her current placement for 10 school days or less in that school year, if services are not provided to a child without disabilities who has been similarly removed.

(4) After a child with a disability has been removed from his or her current placement for 10 school days in the same school year, if the current removal is for not more than 10 consecutive school days and is not a change of placement under § 300.536, school personnel, in consultation with at least one of the child's teachers, determine the extent to which services are needed under paragraph (d)(1) of this section, if any, and the location in which services, if any, will be provided.

(5) If the removal is for more than 10 consecutive school days or is a change of placement under § 300.536, the child's IEP Team determines appropriate services under paragraph (d)(1) of this section and the location in which services will be provided.

(e) *Manifestation determination.* (1) Except for removals that will be for not more than 10 consecutive school days and will not constitute a change of placement under § 300.536, within 10 school days of any decision to change the placement of a child with a disability because of a violation of a code of student conduct, the LEA, the parent, and relevant members of the child's IEP Team (as determined by the parent and the LEA) must review all relevant information in the student's file, including the child's IEP, any teacher observations, and any relevant information provided by the parents to determine—

(i) If the conduct in question was caused by, or had a direct and substantial relationship to, the child's disability; or

(ii) If the conduct in question was the direct result of the LEA's failure to implement the IEP.

(2) The conduct must be determined to be a manifestation of the child's disability if the LEA, the parent, and relevant members of the child's IEP Team determine that a condition in either paragraph (e)(1)(i) or (1)(ii) of this section was met.

(f) *Determination that behavior was a manifestation.* If the LEA, the parent, and relevant members of the IEP Team make the determination that the conduct was a manifestation of the child's disability, the IEP Team must—

(1) Either—

(i) Conduct a functional behavioral assessment, unless the LEA had conducted a functional behavioral assessment before the behavior that resulted in the change of placement occurred, and implement a behavioral intervention plan for the child; or

(ii) If a behavioral intervention plan already has been developed, review the behavioral intervention plan, and modify it, as necessary, to address the behavior; and

(2) Except as provided in paragraph (g) of this section, return the child to the placement from which the child was removed, unless the parent and the LEA agree to a change of placement as part of the modification of the behavioral intervention plan.

(g) *Special circumstances.* School personnel may remove a student to an interim alternative educational setting for not more than 45 school days without regard to whether the behavior is determined to be a manifestation of the child's disability, if the child—

(1) Carries a weapon to or possesses a weapon at school, on school premises, or to or at a school function under the jurisdiction of an SEA or an LEA;

(2) Knowingly possesses or uses illegal drugs, or sells or solicits the sale of a controlled substance, while at school, on school premises, or at a school function under the jurisdiction of an SEA or an LEA; or

(3) Has inflicted serious bodily injury upon another person while at school, on school premises, or at a school function under the jurisdiction of an SEA or an LEA.

(h) *Notification.* Not later than the date on which the decision to take disciplinary action is made, the LEA must notify the parents of that decision, and provide the parents the procedural safeguards notice described in § 300.504.

(i) *Definitions.* For purposes of this section, the following definitions apply:

(1) *Controlled substance* means a drug or other substance identified under schedules I, II, III, IV, or V in section 202(c) of the Controlled Substances Act (21 U.S.C. 812(c)).

(2) *Illegal drug* means a controlled substance; but does not include a controlled substance that is legally possessed or used under the supervision of a licensed healthcare professional or that is legally possessed or used under any other authority under that Act or under any other provision of Federal law.

(3) *Serious bodily injury* has the meaning given the term "serious bodily injury" under paragraph (3) of subsection (h) of section 1365 of title 18, United States Code.

(4) *Weapon* has the meaning given the term "dangerous weapon" under paragraph (2) of the first subsection (g) of section 930 of title 18, United States Code.
(Authority: 20 U.S.C. 1415(k)(1) and (7))

§ 300.531   Determination of setting.

The interim alternative educational setting referred to in § 300.530(c) and (g) is determined by the IEP Team.
(Authority: 20 U.S.C. 1415(k)(2))

§ 300.532 Appeal.

(a) *General.* The parent of a child with a disability who disagrees with any decision regarding placement under §§ 300.530 and 300.531, or the manifestation determination under § 300.530(e), or an LEA that believes that maintaining the current placement of the child is substantially likely to result in injury to the child or others, may request a hearing.

(b) *Authority of hearing officer.* (1) A hearing officer under § 300.511 hears, and makes a determination regarding, an appeal requested under paragraph (a) of this section.

(2) In making the determination under paragraph (b)(1) of this section, the hearing officer may—

(i) Return the child with a disability to the placement from which the child was removed if the hearing officer determines that the removal was a violation of § 300.530 or that the child's behavior was a manifestation of the child's disability; or

(ii) Order a change of placement of the child with a disability to an appropriate interim alternative educational setting for not more than 45 school days if the hearing officer determines that maintaining the current placement of the child is substantially likely to result in injury to the child or to others.

(3) The procedures under paragraphs (a) and (b)(1) and (2) of this section may be repeated, if the LEA believes the child would be dangerous if returned to the original placement.

(c) *Expedited hearing.* (1) Whenever a hearing is requested under paragraph (a) of this section, the parents or the LEA involved in the dispute must have an opportunity for an impartial due process hearing consistent with the requirements of §§ 300.510 through 300.514, except as provided in paragraph (c)(2) through (5) of this section.

(2) The SEA or LEA must arrange for an expedited hearing, which must occur within 20 school days of the date the hearing is requested and must result in a determination within 10 school days after the hearing.

(3) Except as provided in § 300.510(a)(3)—

(i) A resolution session meeting must occur within seven days of the date the hearing is requested, and

(ii) The hearing may proceed unless the matter has been resolved to the satisfaction of both parties within 15 days of receipt of the hearing request.

(4) For an expedited hearing, a State may provide that the time periods identified in § 300.512(a)(3) and (b) are not less than two business days.

(5) A State may establish different procedural rules for expedited hearings under this section than it has established for due process hearings under §§ 300.511 through 300.513.

(6) The decisions on expedited due process hearings are appealable consistent with § 300.514.

(Authority: 20 U.S.C. 1415(k)(3) and (4)(B), 1415(f)(1)(A))

§ 300.533 Placement during appeals.

When an appeal under § 300.532 has been requested by either the parent or the LEA, the child must remain in the interim alternative educational setting pending the decision of the hearing officer or until the expiration of the time period provided for in § 300.530(c) or (g), whichever occurs first, unless the parent and the SEA or LEA agree otherwise.

(Authority: 20 U.S.C. 1415(k)(4)(A))

§ 300.534 Protections for children not yet eligible for special education and related services.

(a) *General.* A child who has not been determined to be eligible for special education and related services under this part and who has engaged in behavior that violated a code of student conduct, may assert any of the protections provided for in this part if the LEA had knowledge (as determined in accordance with paragraph (b) of this section) that the child was a child with a disability before the behavior that precipitated the disciplinary action occurred.

(b) *Basis of knowledge.* An LEA must be deemed to have knowledge that a child is a child with a disability if before the behavior that precipitated the disciplinary action occurred—

(1) The parent of the child expressed concern in writing to supervisory or administrative personnel of the appropriate educational agency, or a teacher of the child, that the child is in need of special education and related services;

(2) The parent of the child requested an evaluation of the child pursuant to §§ 300.300 through 300.311; or

(3) The teacher of the child, or other personnel of the LEA, expressed specific concerns about a pattern of behavior demonstrated by the child directly to the director of special education of the agency or to other supervisory personnel of the agency in accordance with the agency's established child find or special education referral system.

(c) *Exception.* A public agency would not be deemed to have knowledge under paragraph (b) of this section if—

(1) The parent of the child—

(i) Has not allowed an evaluation of the child pursuant to §§ 300.300 through 300.311; or

(ii) Has refused services under this part; or

(2) The child has been evaluated and determined to not be a child with a disability under this part.

(d) *Conditions that apply if no basis of knowledge.* (1) If an LEA does not have knowledge that a child is a child with a disability (in accordance with paragraphs (b) and (c) of this section) prior to taking disciplinary measures against the child, the child may be subjected to the disciplinary measures applied to children without disabilities who engaged in comparable behaviors consistent with paragraph (d)(2) of this section.

(2)(i) If a request is made for an evaluation of a child during the time period in which the child is subjected to disciplinary measures under § 300.530, the evaluation must be conducted in an expedited manner.

(ii) Until the evaluation is completed, the child remains in the educational placement determined by school authorities, which can include suspension or expulsion without educational services.

(iii) If the child is determined to be a child with a disability, taking into consideration information from the evaluation conducted by the agency and information provided by the parents, the agency must provide special education and related services in accordance with this part, including the requirements of §§ 300.530 through 300.536 and section 612(a)(1)(A) of the Act.

(Authority: 20 U.S.C. 1415(k)(5))

§300.535 Referral to and action by law enforcement and judicial authorities.

(a) *Rule of construction.* Nothing in this part prohibits an agency from reporting a crime committed by a child with a disability to appropriate authorities or prevents State law enforcement and judicial authorities from exercising their responsibilities with regard to the application of Federal and State law to crimes committed by a child with a disability.

(b) *Transmittal of records.* (1) An agency reporting a crime committed by a child with a disability must ensure that copies of the special education and disciplinary records of the child are transmitted for consideration by the appropriate authorities to whom the agency reports the crime.

(2) An agency reporting a crime under this section may transmit copies of the child's special education and disciplinary records only to the extent that the transmission is permitted by the Family Educational Rights and Privacy Act.

(Authority: 20 U.S.C. 1415(k)(6))

The specific information pertaining to the change of placement and whether there is a pattern of removals that constitutes a pattern is in Section 300.536.

§ 300.536 Change of placement because of disciplinary removals.

For purposes of removals of a child with a disability from the child's current educational placement under §§300.530 through 300.535, a change of placement occurs if—

(a) The removal is for more than 10 consecutive school days; or

(b) The child has been subjected to a series of removals that constitute a pattern—

(1) Because the series of removals total more than 10 school days in a school year;

(2) Because the child's behavior, if (sic) substantially similar to the child's behavior in the incidents that resulted in the series of removals, taken cumulatively, is determined, under § 300.530(f), to have been a manifestation of the child's disability; and

(3) Because of such additional factors as the length of each removal, the total amount of time the child has been removed, and the proximity of the removals to one another.

(Authority: 20 U.S.C. 1415(k))

Section 615 (k) discusses the authority of school personnel when considering an order to make a change of placement for a violation of the student code of conduct. This section also discusses the continuation of services, a manifestation determination, special circumstances, an appeal and protections. You may view this document, as well as all other Department of Education documents published in the Federal Register, at the following Web site: www.ed.gov/news/fedregister.